I See Myself, Therefore I Am

I See Myself, Therefore I Am

Pina Di Cola

Gotham Books
30 N Gould St.
Ste. 20820, Sheridan, WY 82801
https://gothambooksinc.com/

Phone: 1 (307) 464-7800

© 2023 Pina Di Cola. All rights reserved.

No part of this book may be reproduced, stored in a retrieval system, or transmitted by any means without the written permission of the author.

Published by Gotham Books (June 23, 2023)

ISBN: 979-8-88775-343-0 (sc)
ISBN: 979-8-88775-344-7 (e)

Because of the dynamic nature of the Internet, any web addresses or links contained in this book may have changed since publication and may no longer be valid.

The views expressed in this work are solely those of the author and do not necessarily reflect the views of the publisher, and the publisher hereby disclaims any responsibility for them.

Contents

Preface · vii

1 Photography as Insight · · · · · · · · · · · · · · · · · · · 1
2 In the Virtual World · 13
    Social Media as Virtual Life · · · · · · · · · · · · · · · · 13
    The Selfie as Virtual Image · · · · · · · · · · · · · · · · 19
3 Seeing Yourself Through Others · · · · · · · · · · · · · 23
    Relying on Other People's Opinions · · · · · · · · · · · 28
4 The Brain's Perception · 37
    How the Brain Perceives the Body · · · · · · · · · · · · 40
    The Visual Process · 42
    How Images Are Created · · · · · · · · · · · · · · · · · 45
5 The Virtual Image in the Mirror · · · · · · · · · · · · · 55
    Lateralization · 63
    Seeing Someone Else in the Mirror · · · · · · · · · · · 66
6 How Mental Images Shape Our Lives · · · · · · · · · · 71
    How to Put the Past Away · · · · · · · · · · · · · · · · · 79
7 The Self as a Visual Self · · · · · · · · · · · · · · · · · · · 81
    The Importance of Self-Image Perception · · · · · · · · 84
    The Self as a Visual Identity · · · · · · · · · · · · · · · · 90
8 Understanding Others to Understand Yourself · · · · · 95
9 Emotions as Images · 101
    The See-Feel Emotions · · · · · · · · · · · · · · · · · · 106
    Emotions vs Feelings · · · · · · · · · · · · · · · · · · · 109

10	It's All in the Face	123
	Noticing Eye Movement	128
	Changing Emotions	130
11	The Photo-Image Process	137
	Self-Knowledge and Photo-Image	139
	Who Should Take Your Photo-Image?	142
	Picturing Your Dreams	144
12	The Photo-Image in Action	151
	Seeing Yourself	155
	About the Author	159
	Bibliography	167

Preface

I KNOW THAT THIS book's title, "I See Myself, Therefore I Am," can be perceived as provocative, but if you pay close attention to the meaning of these words, you will agree that they describe the reality we are living in as individuals and as a society.

When the French philosopher René Descartes wrote "I think, therefore I am" in his *Discourse on Method and the Meditations* in 1637, he introduced the concept of the separation of mind and body; the "Cartesian Dualism." Descartes's concept of the "individual self" is an explanation of what exactly it means to exist. I am alive because I think. I think because I am alive. If I don't think, I am dead. He stated, "I think, therefore I am," meaning that thinking is the one thing that can prove one's existence. Through being conscious and having thoughts is how we know we exist.

As the world transformed around the so-called Scientific Revolution, the seventeenth century proved the right time for Descartes to define his fundamental thoughts about the importance of rational thinking over the perception of the five senses. Ensuing thought revolutions and innovations in many sectors throughout the past four centuries have brought us to this point in history where our lives are shaped daily by technological tools, giving way to virtual realities, such as the internet and social media. The result is the expansion of the visual content we use to express and identify ourselves. Various images—graphic and photographic, professional and amateur, serious and trendy—are extensively circulated online and broadcast literally all over the world. We now feel existence in *appearing* and *being seen*. Were Descartes here today, he would join me in saying, "I see myself, therefore I am."

Working as a celebrity portrait photographer has allowed me to observe people through the camera lens, which inspired me to thoroughly examine human nature and, in particular, our relationship with our self-image. I've discovered through the years that the lack of a clear understanding of the concept of self-image has an impact on our daily life. The key to having a positive self-image is to *see* it clearly, and I have found that this can be achieved through photography.

Relying largely on my own research and professional experience, this book depicts what I learned throughout my career, which led me to realize that self-knowledge is neglected and unexplored and that an accurate visual medium is needed. Face after face has stood before me, and with one look I was able to understand the feelings and needs behind another's expression. I put all my effort into understanding my clients, and learning from them has given me a precious experience that led me to collect, gather, and bring together information to create the concept of Photo-Image.

My interest in the psychology of self, combined with my professional experience, has given me a unique insight into how we see ourselves and how others see us, which greatly impacts the way we live our lives. It was a necessity for me to blend together the concept of the photograph as an object with the abstract concept of the self. That is why I created the Photo-Image process, which allows you to visually project your true self onto a photographic image. This results in an amazing breakthrough that allows the subject to *see* themselves, thereby assessing their needs, wants, and ultimate goals, resulting in an incomparable determination to bring out and achieve their purpose.

To further support the concepts explored at length, this book also includes a detailed analysis of mirror studies and how we perceive our own reflections, how we see each other, and how photography can be used to accurately see ourselves for who we are. Knowing about the illusion of the reflection of mirrors and how the brain functions to perceive images, the significance of emotions attached to images, analyzing facial expressions, and interpreting what others think of us are all essential tools in seeing the real self, but they are not the only ones.

Now, more than ever before, our visual presence holds great importance. Everyone, from kids to the elderly, in even the most remote parts of the world, can have a phone that does anything from taking high-resolution pictures to stream videos at any time. From silly selfies to spectacular photography, we document and share our lives, which generates an unbelievable amount of visual information. The source and destination of most of that information is, of course, a new reality we can log onto: our social media platforms.

When we pull out our phones and open a social media app, we are looking for a break from whatever else is going on in the real world. We might post silly selfies or scroll through dozens of photos that show up on your feed. Though the expectation is a fun, relaxing time away from reality, time spent on these social platforms can have the opposite effect on us. Our encounters on social media can instead leave us feeling isolated and lonely. It is painfully easy to forget to enjoy life with our own eyes when we are focused on displaying it on social media. The never-ending search for the perfect selfie can easily distract us from experiences we should be present for.

Although only a few people go to that extent, it is hard to deny the impact social media and other sources of visual information have on our self-image. We are in a constant battle between our image and other people's—comparing ourselves to the often unreal and highly edited appearances of those who showcase themselves online. As humans, we are naturally competitive beings. What social media does is make it easier to compare your life to other people's lives, which can, and does, take a toll on our mental health. We base our happiness on how we are doing compared to others. We base our well-being on something that is completely out of our control.

By understanding the concepts in this book, you will see that the Photo-Image is an important device for the brain to enable us to see and operate with more information about the total aspect of ourselves. I hope to provide the reader with the necessary knowledge to apply the information I share here, so that you can finally understand the importance of your image and begin your journey to your ideal self, provided by the Photo-Image. Your Photo-Image is a constant reminder to focus on discovering yourself and your truest dreams and also on giving yourself the necessary courage to begin your journey and to do whatever it takes to get there.

The prevailing truth is that one must trust the self, and that trust is gained through self-understanding. You must rely on understanding the self in order to achieve the goals and desires that are unique to you. Knowing what you want can be a battle, but only because there are many pressures, internal and external, that obscure our knowledge. I believe that our minds have the capacity to know what they want and need in order to be happy. Self-discovery is the key that unlocks this reality.

I preface the book now with Epictetus's words that have survived time and doubt and through relentless relevance express what the Photo-Image is sure to inspire; through it, you look into your true self.

"Now is the time to get serious about living your ideals. Once you have determined the spiritual principles you wish to exemplify, abide by these rules as if they were laws, as if it were indeed sinful to compromise them. Don't mind if others don't share your convictions. How long can you afford to put off who you really want to be? Your nobler self cannot wait any longer.

"Put your principles into practice—now. Stop the excuses and procrastination. This is your life! You aren't a child anymore. The sooner you set yourself to your spiritual program, the happier you will be. The longer you wait, the more you will be vulnerable to mediocrity and feel filled with shame and regret, because you know you are capable of better.

"From this instant on, vow to stop disappointing yourself. Separate yourself from the mob. Decide to be extraordinary and do what you need to do—now."

1

Photography as Insight

We are currently living in the Visual Age, surrounded by an ever-growing amount of visual technology. We can't deny that multimedia and auiovisual content is a constant element in our daily lives. With this comes an unprecedented phenomenon: the collective need to display our own image in order to become one with the world around us.

Despite our habit of constantly showing our image, we are still unable to truly see ourselves. Now, more than ever, it is important to understand the foundation of this universal problem, and the physics behind our inability to see our own image, which lets the opinions of others control our lives. This is our biggest struggle in life: we can see everything in the world except our own selves. This creates a lot of confusion in our brains, giving rise to emotions and behaviors that we don't understand. This hindrance makes us use social media and the opinions of others as a mirror—as a tool to create our own understanding of ourselves.

My understanding of the importance of images in our lives comes from personal experience. I have spent my entire life learning the nature of visual representations to understand the reality of how we see ourselves, how others see us, and our constant search for the ideal image.

Throughout my career, I've heard it all:
"I'm not photogenic."
"I don't look good in pictures."
"I'm camera shy."
"Don't take pictures of me from this side."
"My nose is too big."
"I'm too fat."
"If I lost weight, maybe then I'd be photogenic."
"When I was a child, I was so photogenic."
"The camera puts ten pounds on me."
That last one is my favorite.

It's this comment that so perfectly illuminates the great problem of self-image: we don't know what we look like.

Our appearance, as we know it, is formed by combining information on how others see us and the opinions they form based on their interpretation of our looks. The visual self, on the other hand, is one's appearance to themselves; it is our own subjective interpretation of our physical appearance through which we recognize ourselves, and it can be very different from what we appear to others. Our visual self can only be seen in our mind's eye and through photography, and it is an important source of information.

During my photoshoots, I started to notice the difference in how people looked at themselves in the mirror, which I propped beside my camera to allow clients to better orient their bodies for the shot, and how they looked through the camera lens. I heard countless complaints about their looks, which compelled me to further my knowledge of self-image. Most of my clients saw them-selves as inadequate, while I saw them as beautiful. It was then that I realized that the "you" in the mirror is not the real "you."

These observations about mirrors and camera lenses prompted the questions:
"How do you see yourself?"
"How do you know what you look like?"
"Why do you think you are not photogenic?"
Each of these questions led me to discover that our brain senses only the

virtual image of ourselves provided by the mirror, not our *real* image. My own research indicates that, because of the way the brain and neurological systems function, you are unable to see your face and body in their totality. Therefore, if you rely only on your reflection in the mirror, you don't know what you really look like. This unique approach has never before been explored.

What you see in the mirror is an inaccurate image of what your brain perceives, and this affects the self-image you form about yourself. By analyzing mirror studies, neurology, emotions, and photography, and recognizing the contributions of great minds in these fields, I have come to the conclusion that, to have a clear and complete understanding of the self, we must first accurately understand self-image.

I say all this as an experienced photographer who, from a very early age, started to reflect on the meaning of photography for our image, how it influences our lives, and how it shaped mine.

The camera has been my best friend since I first entered a darkroom at school when I was fifteen. I saw magic before my eyes when I immersed a piece of white paper in a liquid solution and a photograph came out. It began as a light shade of gray, which turned darker and darker until an image was finally revealed, and I saw a human face!

I went to one of the first high schools in Italy that offered visual art programs: Graphic Design, Publicity, and of course, Photography. I was the only girl in a class of fifteen students, and my friends would constantly make fun of me for choosing to study *Fotografia Artistica*, which had always been reserved for boys.

After school, nobody wanted to hire me. First, because of my age. I was far too young! Second, because I didn't have any real-life experience as a photographer. I had just graduated, and my portfolio only consisted of school projects. Most of all, though, nobody wanted to hire me because I was a woman. Every single person I approached to ask for a job would laugh skepti-cally and would make sarcastic remarks about my work. I heard "I told you so!" countless times from family and friends, and I very nearly gave up. Since photo studios would laugh me out the door, I decided to call every photog-rapher in the yellow pages.

That's when I found somebody listed under the letter *P* by the name of Praturlon, who I thought was a foreign photographer. He took a chance on me and asked me to come in for an interview a few days later. I was over the moon!

When I arrived at the building for the interview, I entered the elevator. There was a beautiful receptionist, and she took me to the director's office. When we got there, I looked around and saw huge, glamorous photos of beau-tiful women hanging on the walls. Once the director arrived, I immediately opened my portfolio and started showing him my photos. I didn't even let him talk, because I thought he would just tell me that he didn't need me. I was think-ing that maybe if he saw my pictures, he would see past my gender and my age and see that I produced good work!

The director, who seemed like a really nice man, looked through my port-folio and called a few of his colleagues to come take a look. As the other men approached, they all started laughing obnoxiously, making rude remarks about my photos. I felt my eyes immediately fill with tears. I felt absolutely humiliated and confused. One of the guys picked up a pile of photos and magazines and handed them to me.

"This is what we do, here, and, if you want, you can be a model, too! You are pretty, and young," he said, as they all laughed.

Those images were all of nude women and could almost be considered porn. I felt not only tears running down my face but also an immense feeling of em-barrassment, since I had never seen such intimate photos of women. When I was finally able to talk, I told them I was looking for Pierluigi Praturlon. Apparently, I was on the wrong floor.

One of the guys, still laughing, escorted me up the stairs to the third floor to Praturlon's studio.

While I still had tears running down my face and could barely talk, the guy told Praturlon the story of what happened, still making fun of me. Pierluigi looked at me, thoughtfully, and felt sorry. He didn't ask to look through my portfolio, but, at that point, I didn't even care. I just wanted to run away. He then asked whether I knew how to print and develop photos, which I did. Right then and there, he sent me to the lab.

Pierluigi Praturlon was a still photographer for movies, and my job was to carry his equipment to set, then standby to reload film. Our first movie togeth-er, *Amarcord*, was directed by "the Maestro," an intimidating man by the name Federico Fellini. I'll never forget when Fellini's assistant asked me to come to the set and shoot while Pierluigi was on a cigarette break. I tried to explain that I couldn't, that I was only the assistant, but he wouldn't hear it; the Maestro needed stills, and he needed them *now*. I panicked. I took Pierluigi's camera and walked into the set. Everyone was staring at me up and down as if I were a freak, except Fellini; he didn't look at me at all. I started shaking uncontrol-lably. I could barely hold the camera. I didn't want them to know that I was inexperienced, and that I had never shot with a Leica in my life. My head was blank. I almost passed out.

Days later, after developing the film, I presented my best shots to the Maestro. He pocketed them.

"Why were you shaking so much?" he asked, "Are you scared of me?"

I said, "Yes," and explained to him that this was my first shoot, and he was amused.

He turned to Pierluigi and said, "The girl can keep shooting so you can go back to smoking."

Everybody laughed. The Maestro had accepted me.

From then on, I was shooting black-and-white for *Amarcord*, and Pierluigi was shooting color and slides. I quickly became really comfortable on set and became friends with all the women on the crew. I took the job very seriously, and Pierluigi now felt confident enough to send me to the set alone when he was busy in his studio. From February until July, I was working mostly by myself.

Watching Fellini work with actors was amazing—he was an artist! Learning from both him and Pierluigi was incredible. My career had finally started, and I could now call myself a photographer.

Ten years (and thirty-five movies) later, I'd learned more about beauty, feel-ings, and emotions through actors' expressions than I thought possible. I spent every scene watching their faces convey emotion: laughter, sadness, joy, heart-break. My role was to capture those feelings for publicity. I began to understand the relationship between the directors and actors. I even became able to dis-tinguish between real emotions and acted expressions. I loved my job, but ten years on strangers' sets was enough. I was ready to create my own scenes on my own set, so I opened a beautiful studio in Rome.

The relationship I had built with my celebrity friends became uncomfortable in my studio. On film sets, the stars were my friends; I saw them as regular people who I'd eat lunch and share frustrations about the times with. However, now, I was in charge, and they were in front of *my* camera in *my* studio. The first photoshoots were difficult: my subjects were skeptical, challenging, and stiff, despite our history. The pictures we took were fine, but the feelings were missing. Either way, I had to make sense of their reactions.

I learned a great lesson: everyone in front of the lens should feel like a VIP. Celebrity or otherwise, a subject should feel admired and light and be able to open up. The celebrities were my friends, and I'd forgotten to treat them like celebrities. I forgot that the reason we took pictures was that their fans wanted to see them in magazines (as the internet and social media were yet to arrive). I changed my strategy to prioritize kindness and respect, and I soon found my work published in prestigious magazines throughout Europe. I became a well-known photographer.

After a week-long vacation in Los Angeles, my mind suddenly shifted. Immediately, I returned to Rome, closed my studio, and sold the lights and equipment because they used a different voltage in America. Without thinking and without ever looking back, I moved to LA. I felt very excited, as my life was going in a new direction. Finding work in LA was easy. I only had to contact agencies, and they'd line up to have their clientele appear in European magazines.

At this point in my career, my goal had become clear: to make everybody beautiful and confident, and to clear away confusion and social anxiety. After so many years of shooting celebrities from all sectors, seeing my photos in glossy magazines no longer satisfied me; bringing out the best in people did—their expressions, their truth, their beauty. The importance of protecting one's essential self dwarfed the price tag of the clothes they wore. At some point, I had realized that my clients' celebrity status no longer mattered to me. All humans were beautiful and worthy of respect and appreciation.

Then, I focused on my pursuit of knowledge. I enrolled in school, where I studied psychology to understand perspectives on the concepts of image and beauty that I wrestled within my head. I studied physics to understand mirrors and how eyes interpret light. This was one of the hardest things I have ever done but, at last, I could reinforce my theories with professional evidence.

No matter where I was—Italy or Los Angeles—I could see my clients struggling with the relationship between insecurity and confidence throughout my entire career and not being able to say anything. The word "photogenic" in particular would always pop up in my career. I still have nightmares about it. The term literally means "genic human figure" and was coined by the pioneer photographer William Fox Talbot (1800–1877). Now, it is used to describe a person who looks good in pictures. It can be discouraging, as it suggests other people naturally look worse in photos, or that someone photogenic looks worse in real life. I often hear people say they aren't photogenic to justify their poor self-esteem. They'll say, "I'm not photogenic!" before taking a picture just to prevent surprise and reinforce a negative self-image. Or, after their picture is taken, they'll say, "I told you I'm not photogenic!" or "It's not me!" Could it be they don't recognize themselves? In my experience, "I'm not photogenic" means "I don't know what I look like."

I once worked with an actress who was one of the most beautiful people I'd ever seen. I could spend hours photographing her face, playing with all types of lighting, poses, and expressions. Her face was beautiful, but as soon as I'd zoom in on her shoulder, or hand, or finger, her beauty would disappear. She had a beautiful, slender body, but her movements were awkward and mechanical. When she moved, her shoulders would collapse, and her pose would change. It felt like her body was dissociated from her face. Her facial expressions would change so drastically that it was impossible to obtain a nice body shot. Despite her beauty, her career never went very far.

I've found that a person's external beauty disappears if it isn't supported by every part of them; a person is a sum of their personality, values, joys, and attitude, including their state of mind. In the case of this beautiful actress, she couldn't achieve true beauty because she couldn't harmonize it with her body.

There's no one theory that defines beauty, but scientists believe it's based on symmetry and lateralization, as defined by the proportion of the left and right sides of a face, and the distances between facial features. Big eyes, glowing skin, and shiny hair throughout history have played a significant role in defining attractiveness, but people can have flaws by conventional standards—an imperfect feature or a blemish—and still possess beauty because of the way they carry themselves, because of who they are as a person. Beauty is a total expression of a person's security, capacity, benevolence, and confidence in themselves that results in a visible harmony; neither a pretty face nor a fit body alone define it.

There have been instances where I've determined natural beauty in my subject's symmetrical face but couldn't capture it. I trusted myself, so I failed to understand that my nuanced perception of beauty wouldn't translate to my images. These were moments when my clients' faces were out of harmony with their internal beauty. It could have been a negative attitude or avoiding eye contact that ruined these pictures, and not so much the defined face line, the position of the head, or the way they moved their mouths, smiled, or angled their shapely eyebrows. This indicates that a person is unsure of how to combine their innate beauty with their other qualities.

If one takes into account only their physical features, they may be disappointed to find that it's exceedingly rare to find perfect symmetry. We often surround ourselves with people that we look at through the lens of our mood, determining beauty or ugliness by our opinions, status, and how we feel at the moment, combined with how others feel at the same time. Little do we expect what the camera reveals. The so-called average face transforms into beauty, and immense pleasure results from this delightful surprise. Their average face has changed, and their personality changes with it to communicate excitement, confidence, and charm. The result is true beauty, because beauty has to come from within.

When you deeply observe someone, you inevitably form a connection with their feelings and expressions. You create a rapport with them. I could never move forward with my work without finding something good about the client—physically or emotionally—and finding their hidden beauty and their best side. There's beauty in all of us, we just sometimes don't see it.

I first realized this at photography school, as the only girl in a class with fourteen young men. Every day, we shot subjects from still-life to nature to people. Finding models was as easy as going into the next room and asking someone to pose. The boys routinely chose the cute girls and left me with the less attractive ones that were a little less eager to be photographed. I was well aware of their imperfections—their acne, their bulky forms. Still, I felt responsible to keep them from feeling inferior to the others picked by the boys.

I know that being in their position is not easy. Everyone in front of a camera, it doesn't matter if they're a regular person or a celebrity, has the same worries and attitudes. We all can get anxious. Even the most famous celebrity! As a photographer, then, I am responsible for setting aside their status and getting into their minds. I have to capture feelings and moods without saying a word. The magic moment for me is when the clients express themselves with a timid attempt to show their best self, and I recognize that moment. Then, the camera disappears from my hands, and the connection with the client is a pleasurable experience for both of us. That's when you know it will be a beautiful photo.

Back at school, I began our sessions by focusing solely on the girls' smiles and expressions, making sure they felt secure with my abundant feedback. I'd entice brilliant smiles and sparkling eyes of eager teenagers looking back at me with confidence. The results amazed me—my photos and my girls were just as beautiful as any of the boys. It's unbelievable what happens when we forget to compare ourselves to others and let go of the fear of their criticism.

No one is perfect, but we can find perfection in anyone if we want to. Ugliness emerges when others only focus on your imperfections—when those people focus on their own problems and reflect their unhappiness onto you. Focus on the good features you possess and know that the bad can probably be fixed if you work hard. To be photogenic is to be in harmony with your body; your flaws will always blend in with your good aspects when your features and face become harmonious.

Celebrities usually come to my studio followed by an entourage—a make-up person, a stylist, and a hairstylist, a manager, and a publicist, and often even a friend or two would tag along. As a result, the celebrity appeared with a full-blown sense of stardom. However, when they are in the studio with me, they leave their celebrity status and reveal their true self. Their status comes off, and the real person is revealed. It is only then that I can establish a rapport with the subject. The strength of the relationship between the subject and photographer, the perception and warm understanding, is why I fell in love with photography. More than a trade, it is a way of seeing that aids my interaction with the world.

Today, with social media websites and phones in our pockets, we are the ones responsible for capturing our image most of the time. The problem is that we are consciously constructing our image in accordance to what we think belongs in the world. Or, more specifically, we are reshaping our lives into a new concept, now called a "virtual identity." The reality is that we don't yet know how to manage this power that allows us to display parts of ourselves and hide others.

The image of the self has become a concern for all of us. Self-concept and, more specifically, self-image and self-esteem issues are unclear to everyone, which can be damaging to our well-being. Therefore, we need to revisit them in a new visual context to understand the role of images in both our lives and other people's as we go through this confusing time.

Through exploring this inability to accurately see what we look like, I developed the concept of Photo-Image. The visual self, provided by the Photo-Image, is a vital piece in completing the idea of the self.

What is a Photo-Image? It is a photograph of your image that reflects your awareness of your total self. "Photo-Image" may sound a little odd at first. I call it this to distinguish it from the many more popular uses and variations of the word "photo." It's a photograph—an image of you—not as a portrait or a snapshot, but as a tangible reality of your essence that you can observe objectively and subjectively. From the Photo-Image, you can gain knowledge of who you are as a person. The qualities and details of your face and body reveal information about the inner self, providing you with a clear, visual interpretation of who you are.

Can we ever be sure of who we are? Until now, your self-image was based mainly on the image others have of you. However, you are *not* the opinion that your friends and coworkers have of you, your wealth or status, or, surprisingly, even the image that you see in the mirror.

Your Photo-Image uniquely allows you to free yourself from the opinion of others, reconnecting you with your inner self, opening your mind's eyes, and finding the truth about who you are that pushes you onward. The power of this exists in the physics of our eyes and brain, on knowing that our brain is physically unable to see our face and body clearly.

Photo-Image, then, is the link to introduce yourself to your brain. It is the quintessence of who you are and what you look like in your mind's eye, with your total consciousness—your capability, identity, beliefs, characteristics, and qualities that only you know and have.

How many times have you thought someone didn't understand you because they didn't know enough about who you are as a person? By using the Photo-Image, we provide the brain with an accurate image of our visual self to better coordinate the ideas of self-concept, self-perception, and the awareness of our being in time and space. Your Photo-Image will help you become sure of who you are and will motivate you to achieve the best for yourself.

In this way, I have been able to use photography as a visual aid toward self-discovery.

I will take a moment to remind you that this book only focuses on the visual system, though language systems also play a vital role in happiness and self-definition. It is almost globally accepted that happiness must come from within. In order to find happiness and self-realization in life, we must first see ourselves and know who we are.

My professional experience and my studies concerning the relationship between images, self-image, the self, beauty, how mirrors work, and the phys-ics behind it all, have taken a lot of work, but I have been determined to find reasons for the struggles with self-confidence I have personally overcome and have seen others go through.

My motivation is to make others feel beautiful and confident in themselves, to make them trust my point of view and my ability to elicit their best self, and to clear the confusion and misunderstanding of how they see themselves based on how other people see them. This became a prevalent theme in my everyday work as a photographer, which lead me to understand how we form incorrect beliefs based on a "beauty standard" developed by the media, and how it can negatively impact our sense of self. Understanding this relationship has made my photoshoots with clients successful and the exploration of feelings to un-cover their true self possible. Of course, I have always taken the reason behind the shoot into consideration, but at some point while shooting, that was not important, anymore. What was important was that my subject was a beautiful human being whom I'll always respect and be grateful for having met.

2

In the Virtual World

Social Media as Virtual Life

We typically base our idea of who we are on how others see us, paired with the reflection we see in the mirror. By doing that, our self-image is being constructed from subjective, external impressions. The absence of having a real image of what we look like creates a lack of self-knowledge that can distort our impression of who we are. Again, to *know* ourselves, we must first *see* ourselves.

As briefly mentioned in the previous chapter, we are now facing the challenge of being the ones responsible for crafting part our own external virtual self, which implies that we have to adapt our images to social trends in order to construct our real inner image of "self." The selfie is a convenient tool used to adjust one's appearance to the way one sees themselves. The selfie is quite possibly the main function of photography today. Its primary purposes are both communication as well as the shaping of the virtual personality, and that is the worrying part.

Every time we log onto Facebook, we are faced with the question: "What is on your mind today?" and we are compelled to answer it. It is like we are being invited to make an entrance on a stage to perform to a massive audience, impersonating and creating a virtual identity with each post. We are compelled to show our presence, and do so in accordance with what our audience seems to like or dislike. We carefully select parts of our lives to display in order to create in others the idea that we want them to have of us. We are actors, and we create our own roles with these fictional identities.

All of this, as you can imagine, takes a lot of energy and time. We are constantly on the verge of anxiety, seeking other people's acknowledgment and approval. Every day, we test how people respond to our image, hopeful that we will receive more "likes" or "hearts" than our friends. We post what we think others want to see. When the flattering remarks come, they make us feel popular and loved. They give us the confirmation that our identity belongs in the world. We finally have proof that people are watching and they approve of us. The moment we post a selfie, we know that we are an important presence in the world—we only become somebody when we share our image.

Social media also leads us to analyze, examine, and dissect every imperfection we can find in our appearance and everybody else's. We increase our anxiety by having unrealistic expectations of what our lives are supposed to look like by comparing them to people's curated images. Ultimately, with every post, we are exposed to criticism and judgment. This can be devastating and the source of many self-image and identity issues.

Through social media platforms, like Instagram and Facebook, we have instant access to billions of people's lives. We are constantly watching others with better lives and more followers than us, and we are sure to find somebody who will make us feel bad about our own, be it because of their beautiful house or their flawless skin. There are people out there whose job is to live an enviable life—to make their life look as beautiful and fun as possible, which often makes their millions of followers end up feeling bad about their own experiences, or lack thereof. That makes us constantly question how to present ourselves online, which in turn creates constant anxiety in our minds.

Sometimes, we construct an imagined self-image that, though we do not recognize, we believe in and depend on. We attempt to be exactly what we think others expect of us, and when we can't—and we never can—we end up feeling miserable.

A person's construction of an imagined self-image is done unintentionally. We are not consciously aware that we often try to conform to the image that we imagine other people expect from us. And if a person develops a negative self-image, their self-esteem will tend to be low. If we think that others' opinions of us are more relevant than our own, we will end up living our lives to make them happy, becoming miserable ourselves and having a weak self-image.

The major problem created by our time spent on social media is the relationship between our image and other people's, which becomes unclear, as well as the blurred line between the real and virtual that creates many issues in how we view ourselves and the world. FOMO (Fear of Missing Out) in particular stands out due to its tangible effects on our daily lives.

Between many of its forms, FOMO can emerge from our need to show ourselves online. If we don't, it is almost as if we didn't exist. To see our images become one with the world around us is the only way we feel real, and this creates in us the endless pressure to stay online. By being online, we are led to consume continuous content of people living seemingly perfect lives, which creates in us a deep-set fear of missing out on not only these experiences, but on watching them. This makes us crave being connected and keeping up to date with what everyone else is up to, even if—most of the time—those things are not at all relevant to us.

As you can see, social platforms sometimes make us replace real-life interactions with time spent in front of a screen simply consuming information. And in this world, where content is coming in from all directions, we start feeling replaceable. We don't want to be online, but we also don't want to get lost in the crowd. If we are not there, who will remember us? If they don't see my image, who am I? We feel as if our presence online is paramount to our significance in the world.

A couple of years ago, I met a young girl named Lia, who was a perfect example of how damaging social media can be if used as a means to know yourself and others.

Lia was around fifteen when she started using social media regularly. She would post pictures of herself and her friends, or selfies. At first, the only people interested were her friends, of course, but more and more people started following her account, partly because of her looks. But Lia actively tries to spread a message of love and gratitude. "The world is full of beautiful people, but I have a brain, and a heart. I want people to see that," says Lia.

In the first few years, she struggled with the popularity; she felt vain. Lia felt as if all those people only cared about a pretty face that probably will make them feel bad about themselves. "I, myself, followed a lot of girls who made me feel bad about myself, and I didn't want to be one of those."

She deleted her Instagram account a few times. She tried to start over and be a normal girl with only friends and family around, but people would always come back. And, by that time, Lia already craved the attention that she would get whenever she posted a selfie . . . So, she decided to make the best of it. Lia started posting regularly to her Instagram feed, which made her follower count skyrocket.

"Brands began to approach me and offer to pay thousands of dollars if I mentioned their names in a post! Every makeup, clothing, and jewelry company wanted to work with me . . . I couldn't believe it!" Lia remembers.

She was going to school for fashion design during that time but didn't have enough time to manage both lives, so she decided to drop out. Instagram had officially become her full-time job.

Slowly, Lia started to realize that she wasn't paying attention to what she was promoting; they weren't always the things she believed in. "I remember opening my feed one day and scrolling through my posts . . . the person I saw wasn't me," she says.

Lia was so excited about this new life that she didn't stop to think about the products she was associating her image with.

"It made me sick to my stomach to see myself promoting fast fashion brands that trick young girls into buying awful products just because people like me pretend to wear them."

Despite not wanting to, Lia continued to promote these brands, due to contracts she had with the companies.

"Fashion design is my one passion in life, so advertising these clothes I hated made me extremely depressed . . . especially knowing that I wasn't following my goals of designing my own."

Of course, working as an influencer was allowing her to live an amazing life. People would pay her to travel, restaurants let her eat for free, and she would never have to spend money on makeup again. And yet, the awareness that she wasn't following her passion, and the pressure of being such a big influence for millions of people, was hard to manage.

"It definitely is hard to control, to not let social media overtake your brain. I went through many phases where I wondered if all of that was worth it."

Lia felt a pressure to post on social media constantly, since that is necessary to maintain any type of success. She realized that it was important to have a life "off camera," but struggled to separate her personal life from her job. She went through stages where the pressure of being the perceived "perfect girl," of living the apparent perfect life became too much.

"People feel entitled. They think that because I post most of my life online, they have the right to comment on my freckles, or on my boyfriend, or whether or not my breakfast was healthy this morning."

She said that it was hard to draw a line, to figure out what things she really wanted to do, and what things she was doing simply because her thousands of followers would want her to do.

"It's hard to maintain your identity, when everyone has an idea of who you should be."

Lia often wondered how long she could do this. She was constantly anxious and even went through bouts of depression when she wanted to give up on everything. Firstly, because she didn't know how long Instagram was going to last.

"Social media networks die all the time, so that's still a fear of mine and of every single person whose lives depend on this."

Secondly, because she didn't feel successful, despite the thousands of likes on her photos.

She would try to distract herself from social media by focusing on her fashion design endeavors, but every single obstacle that appeared in front of Lia ended up paralyzing her, and she would go back running to social media where she felt safe, though incomplete.

"Things came quite easily to me on social media, and they came because of two things I don't really have any control over, which are my looks and how I see the world around me."

The thought of failing while trying to do something she really cared about, and which depended on skills instead of looks, was enough to stop her from trying at all. Instead, she kept promoting fashion brands she hated while living a life that was becoming increasingly frustrating.

Lia heard about my Photo-Image photography service through one of my celebrity clients. When she arrived for her session, I didn't know much about her. She just looked like a very young girl who was self-aware and confident in herself. As we talked, I started learning about her life and about an amazing lifestyle that wasn't very familiar to me. She was living a life that most people are jealous of: traveling, going to good restaurants and unbelievable events, and getting paid to do all of that, but she was still missing something that was a crucial part of who she is.

As we dug deeper, Lia acknowledged that most of her discomfort came from the fact that she had given up on her lifelong dream of being a fashion designer, and she couldn't find the time to focus on her own needs in the midst of the social media show her life had become. Her job as an influencer took away all of her energy, and she was left empty, despite the number of followers and the amount of money it gave her.

As we talked about her goals, she started realizing that her life as an influencer might be an advantage. She noticed that by posting photos of herself in thousands of different outfits and analyzing the number of likes and comments in each of those photos, she could gain an insight into what women want and don't want in the fashion industry. She unknowingly became an expert on something that would give her a huge advantage in an industry she wasn't yet a part of.

By the end of our session, she had questioned everything about her current situation and had already started making a path toward her ideal life. She suddenly understood that her life as an influencer was momentary, and that rid her of all the anxiety she felt about posting constantly, and the number of likes her photos get, and whether her follower count was going up or down.

Her future was crystal clear. She decided to balance her time between her two conflicting passions. She would take two days off social media per week to focus on her new fashion projects. She would no longer accept any clients that she didn't believe in, since now she was in the financial position to do so. She would only promote brands that she personally used and loved. She would be able to maintain her status and her income but would also feel fulfilled.

Lia realized that her job as an influencer would help jumpstart her fashion design brand, just like the brand would give her followers more content. Lia left the photoshoot feeling accomplished and motivated for the first time in a long while. She called me a few months later to thank me for opening her eyes to who she really is.

As you can see from Lia's story, social media can be a battlefield even for those who look like they have it figured out. It can confuse us and distract us, deeply damaging our self-image.

Despite all of this, social media is not a harmful tool; it is only the mirror of ourselves. The reality is that we don't yet know how to manage the power of this new visual technology—how to interact with and use our image in relation to others. It is constructed to define our personal identity, but it also mirrors our need to belong. If we do not engage with social media, we will feel that we are not represented in the world. If cutting social media out is not the answer, then what we must do is reflect on our relationship with ourselves, others, and society. If we don't, our own image, and, therefore, our sense of identity, is at stake.

The Selfie as Virtual Image

We don't often think about where the need to see our own image comes from, or about its importance in our lives. With the ease of access to high definition cameras in today's world, the selfie is becoming people's favorite way to analyze their image. I would like to, once and for all, explain why they have become the phenomenon that we see today, and how they affect our perceptions of ourselves.

We need to know who we are in order to form our identities, and our image is a big part of that. We need to see an object to understand it, and the brain cannot accept that we see others while we are unable to see ourselves (due to the structure of our brains).

Because the mirror isn't accurate and others' opinions shouldn't be taken into consideration, the selfie becomes a substitute for the mirror in interpreting our own face. We unconsciously take selfie after selfie, trying to grasp the idea of who we are, our identity, and therefore our own self.

Think about how this issue has been a part of the "unconscious" human condition, since we first saw our own reflections in pools of water, like lakes and rivers, which naturally didn't accurately represent our images. For this reason, our sense of personal identity didn't exist. For a long time, we thought of ourselves only as part of communities.

Then, from our need to see our image, the first mirrors started being made from polished stones and metals, thousands of years ago, in places like Turkey, Egypt, and China. Metal mirrors were incredibly expensive, so they were only available to the wealthy and the ruling classes. With the discovery of glass making, the Romans started producing mirrors that consisted of mostly glass, with a thin layer of metal. This art was later perfected by the Germans in the 1800s. These glass mirrors were much cheaper to produce, so they slowly became more accessible to the common people. As that happened, there was a shift in society—we could finally see ourselves as individuals, as our own person.

At the same time, the concept of Individualism was born during the Renaissance. This was also when the first self-portraits were being painted, since people could finally see their images clearly. From Parmigianino's *Self Portrait in a Convex Mirror* in 1524 to Van Gogh's famous self-portraits in the 1800s, it is undeniable that the need to see our image, and to show it, has been ever present. The painted self-portrait and the selfie are both based on our desire to document a part of ourselves that is ephemeral. In contrast to selfies, paintings are more open to subjective interpretation of how the artists sees themselves, which is not true for photographs.

The first photographic self-portrait, taken by Robert Cornelius in 1839, came only thirteen years after the invention of photography. The process of documenting yourself in order to create and understand your significance in the world suddenly became much more accessible—it didn't require weeks of work or hundreds of dollars spent on oil paints. All that was needed was a camera.

However, until about twenty years ago, the selfie wasn't as easily attainable as it is today, due to both the physics of analog cameras—like the size of the lens and its focal length—and the price of film and processing, simply turning the camera on yourself and documenting your every move wasn't easy. Selfies like the ones we see today existed, of course, but they seemed to be reserved for important events and memorable moments.

The rise of the digital camera, which enabled us to have a camera in our pockets at any given time, made turning the camera onto ourselves much easier. Unconsciously, the selfie is a photograph that our brain needs, in order to understand what we look like at any time. It acts like a mirror, but it is a photograph that can manipulate the idea that your brain has of yourself with every shot. When we take a selfie, we want to create and invent ourselves. We want to see ourselves as individuals in an ocean of others.

Technically speaking, the selfie is a distorted representation of your face. We don't notice our bigger noses, larger foreheads, and smaller chins, which are the most pronounced features at the angle of the shot. Let us take a closer look at your front-facing camera. If you have one, open it up and assume your favorite selfie-taking position. On most phones, you'll see your image reflected on the screen. You may or may not like what you see. Either way, you'll likely make an immediate judgment that the face in the phone is a credible source of what you look like. Once you take a picture and look at it, you'll see a different version of your face that may be better or worse. Why is that? You haven't changed a thing. All you have is the single freeze-frame of yourself, as a real photo, stuck in time with distorted features from a wide-angle lens. If you flip your camera and take a photo with the rear-facing lens, you'll see a totally different person. In your subconscious mind, your first view is what you'll believe your look is. When you see an image of yourself change, your perception of your reality changes with it, and your inaccurate idea of your personal beauty and defects hurts the way you see yourself.

Look at this selfie you just took. How would you feel if it was posted on all of your social media accounts right now? You, like most people, are probably terrified at the thought, and you fear being judged when you aren't looking your best. Many people do the habitual photo-retouching before posting a selfie, but many are going as far as getting plastic surgeries to look better in selfies. According to the American Society of Plastic Surgeons, selfie rhinoplasty (a minimally invasive procedure designed to retouch the nose and enhance satisfaction in selfies) is becoming alarmingly popular.

All of this impact, simply because people don't understand exactly how the process of taking a selfie works. The fact of the matter is that jumping to conclusions about who you are based on a selfie is dangerous and damaging to both your self-image and your self-esteem, especially during the teenage years, where identities develop and self-images are formed. The problem of the brain not having an accurate image of what you look like is the problem of self-image and its importance, and that is what this book explores at length.

While the reflection in the mirror provides us with a fleeting image (think of how many times you've posed and made a face to alter your reflection in the mirror; it's probably difficult to recall), the selfie is a photograph—a distorted but concrete image that includes negative thoughts such as "I'm not photogenic" or "I'm ugly," or whatever feelings you've attached to that photo. These thoughts become feelings that are registered in your visual cortex and thus become mental images of yourself that are stored away for recall at any time, just waiting to ruin your mood. You'll become dependent on this false image as a reference point for knowing what you look like, edging yourself closer and closer to making a call to the local plastic surgeon.

After reading this, you may think that I'm completely against taking selfies. I'm not. I believe selfies can still be used as a means toward self-discovery, a way to see yourself, and overall, a fun way to connect with friends. Since younger people are in a lot of ways still getting to know themselves, I recommend teens to take group photos instead of taking too many selfies.

Attention to detail goes a long way when taking selfies. Pay attention to the light reflection in your facial features. If it's too harsh, choose a softer shade of light. Many of my friends take selfies in their cars. You'll find the glass and light bouncing off the dashboard creates a much softer, warmer light that softens your features and makes you look better.

I suggest practicing these safe selfies in order to understand the concepts of how your camera works. Practice will give you an awareness of how to better pose for yourself and your friends. Just be sure to remember that selfies aren't accurate representations of your face. Instead of showing your selfies to your followers, keep them for yourself. This may not increase your online popularity, but it'll help your brain process the different sides of yourself that you need in order to form a clear image of who you are.

3

Seeing Yourself Through Others

Our social interactions are often defined by our physical appearance. Besides your close friends and family, it's almost impossible for anyone to know who you really are. We can only show them with our appearance and the items we use to define ourselves. Some of us use makeup, flamboyant behaviors, or even plastic surgery, so that we can distort or transform our body image to provoke others to admire and praise us. Regardless of our technique, we strive to be *somebody* in the eyes of those around us. We become so caught up in the search for acceptance that, in the end, we're too confused to understand what motivates the choices we make. Are we motivated to succeed for our own benefit or for the admiration of others? For what do we make choices? Is it money, fame, love or approval?

For a long time, I worked on movie sets, where—creating and arranging and making believe—everything is possible. All of that is often done with perfect realism. It can be difficult to decide what is real or not, if the actors are telling the truth or being their character. This is not too different from real life and our society. For every social setting we find ourselves in—church, work, school, parties—we wear a different mask, act a different way, and carefully create an attitude and look that belongs in that setting. We craft our self-image. We forget to consider the negative effects that this can have on ourselves.

When we present ourselves to others, we show them our best qualities, our achievements, and we wait for their nonverbal approval that we're good people. In public, we need to put on a big show, and we act as if on a stage. We create stories to impress others, demanding acceptance in the form of respect and consideration. We have to prove our expectations of ourselves to those around us. They know what we want more than we do because we communicate with our appearance, talk, and expressions. How do they know? Because they play the same game, just like us. Everyone is the star of their own movie.

So, we create our mask depending on the role we want to play. We carefully choose our clothes, makeup, accessorize, and style ourselves. We control our gestures to mimic our desires. We're skilled at this. Theoretically, this should result in us attaining what we wanted. This happens everywhere in society, regardless of our social status. Understanding our need to act for others will help us understand where our ambition comes from and how we associate it with our need for approval.

We project our insecurities in a way none of us completely understand. Why do we say what we do and act the way we do? We lock in our perception of self. It is important, however, that we don't allow others to control our feelings or ever risk putting them in a position of influence over our lives. We analyze people's motivations, searching for trust to avoid the risk of being controlled. If we're aware enough to act only for ourselves, we complicate our self-image by mixing it with paranoia, letting it define us. We're tacit as we complicate our identities. We dig into our beliefs—the parts of ourselves that give us the approval we need—as we cling to a confused self-image.

The biggest problem with lack of clarity is that we reject it ourselves. Whether we are destitute or fit, rich, and famous, we'll always feel anxious, because our search for approval goes on forever. If we never quit acting, we'll never be satisfied. Our bodies always tell us when we're acting against our own good, so we build a false foundation for ourselves that we base off what we think others expect us to do. I emphasize the need to understand this concept: awareness of our interaction with others and what we try to convince ourselves to believe about who we are.

Andrew's story is a perfect example of just how far we can go when trying to impress others and please our confused selves.

Andrew was a handsome guy when we met. Truly, his face was nearly perfect. He had beautiful blonde hair, stunning blue eyes, and a beautiful body. I knew his story needed to be told, so I met with him recently over coffee to ask him some questions about his fascinating past.

He grew up in a rural town on the East Coast and was raised by his constructor father and by his stay-at-home mother, who was a former hairdresser. I asked him if she was the reason he decided to become a hairstylist and makeup artist, but he wasn't sure.

"I think I only went to makeup school because it was the closest school to our farm," he laughed.

Everybody at the school was obsessed with him and his beautiful face, and the constant attention reinforced his belief that he was going to be famous one day. That is a thought he had fostered since he was a kid—he knew he was going to be famous, though he didn't know why, when, or how.

"I just knew it."

One day, an important hairdresser came to his school for a seminar, and Andrew got to meet the guy, who turned out to be Tony, a famous celebrity salon owner in Beverly Hills. Tony loved Andrew's work ethic and animated energy, so he later invited him to move out to Los Angeles to work at one of his Beverly Hills salons.

"I was eighteen years old. I couldn't believe what was happening! Me, leaving my farm to be a makeup artist in Los Angeles?! What kind of joke was that?"

Not having to think twice about it, Andrew packed up his things and said goodbye to his family. His new life in Los Angeles was nothing short of thrilling—he was doing hair and makeup for celebrities at the salon, and he felt like his life was heading in the right direction. Everyone he met was immediately charmed by his good looks and fun, lively personality, not to mention his impeccable talent with makeup.

One day, a famous plastic surgeon came to the salon to get his hair done, and after talking to Andrew for a while, he asked him out for drinks. Andrew said yes, and he didn't think much of it. As soon as they sat down and started talking that night, the guy asked Andrew whether he would be open to the idea of getting a chin implant and chin dimple.

"First of all, what?!" he remembered, laughing. "That was the single strangest question anyone has ever asked me."

The surgeon explained to him that this was a trial surgery for Michael Jackson, and that he would be paid $20,000. Andrew was in.

He met with Michael Jackson before and after the surgery so that he could see the progress. The two of them became quite close, and Andrew felt like he was living the life of his dreams. A few months later, they asked him to get a rhinoplasty for Michael, again for $20,000, and he did. Then, biceps. I asked him why he accepted to do so many surgeries on his already-beautiful face.

"It was a lot of money. But I also I love Michael and felt that if Michael could do this and be successful, I could be successful, too . . ."

Meanwhile, celebrities started calling Andrew to ask him to do their make-up and hair, whenever they were doing photoshoots or going on TV. That made Tony jealous, and eventually led to Andrew leaving the salon altogether.

"I don't think he liked the fact that a lot of clients actually preferred me."

By then, he was more available to work for me on photoshoots, so quitting didn't make much of a difference to him.

Andrew had a few more surgeries done, like his cheekbone and neck.

"I started liking what I was seeing in the mirror, you know? I was looking more masculine, and I loved that," he recalled.

At this point, he was thirty-two years old and started seeing signs of aging around his eyes and forehead, which made him freak out. For someone who was always being complimented on his beauty and perfect face, the thought of losing that was nerve-racking. So, Andrew became obsessed with retouching his face. This time for himself. First, he got implants on his forehead, lips, and cheeks. Then, his ears, chest, and eyebrows.

"Every plastic surgery you can think of, I had it done."

One day, he asked me if I could take some photos of him after a photoshoot we worked on together. I accepted, of course. He went to the dressing room and came out with a military-like outfit, and I realized that he was impersonating Michael Jackson. I thought he was only dressing up for the photos, so I didn't think much of it.

The next time we worked together, and many times after, Andrew showed up with long, pitch-black hair, which looked very strange against his naturally fair skin and blue eyes. His face was swollen, full of Botox. It was always unnerving for me to see him like that. I tried to reassure my celebrity clients that he was an excellent makeup artist, but they found it hard to believe that Andrew, who looked like *that*, would make them look good. Some didn't even want him to touch their faces. Eventually, I had to stop calling him to work with me, because he was making everyone uncomfortable.

After a while, even Andrew couldn't stand to look in the mirror and see his own face.

He said, "One day, I wanted to be Michael . . . and the next I wanted to disappear."

Andrew told me he was struggling with depression at that time. He realized the surgeries had become a true obsession for him. He had dozens of surgeries, and though he felt successful in life—working with world-famous celebrities doing something he loves—he wasn't happy, because he wasn't *famous* yet.

"That's when I realized that plastic surgeries were my gateway to fame!"

Andrew finally got his short, blonde hair back, and surgeries became a habit for him.

"People were paying me to have them done, and I knew that I was already beautiful, so why not?" He stopped for a second. "Besides, I became popular because of them. I finally had something to talk about. I was finally interesting to people!"

Andrew became so popular that he was interviewed by E! News, Larry King, and The View . . . he became known for his surgeries and funny celebrity stories, and he even did tours in Europe and all over the US. I asked him how he feels, looking at himself in the mirror.

"I still see myself as beautiful . . ." he said, before pausing and looking directly at me. "But I'm not stupid. I know what people feel when they look at me. I can tell by their facial expressions. After sixty-two procedures, the only thing original left is my blue eyes. But I can't go back now, can I?"

He continued, "I stopped getting surgeries ten years ago. There's nothing more to be done, anyway. I rarely look in the mirror, but when I do, I don't recognize myself. I get a punch to my stomach when I think, 'What have I done?' Soon after, I'll remember feeling beautiful and happy inside, like when I was twenty and promised myself I'd be famous. I think my mindset was always something like, 'If I don't have these plastic surgeries, who am I?' I needed to be famous for something, right?"

Relying on Other People's Opinions

It isn't uncommon for people to base their self-image on what others say about them. Why do we do that? The answer lies within our self-image and will provide a renewed meaning about ourselves and our overall social interactions.

Most of us feel an insatiable desire to know how others perceive us. This desire is so strong that it is impossible to avoid it. Our image of the self, combined with the image others have of us, is a method we instinctively use to develop our overall self-image. Our minds allow our body-images to become an object in the eyes of others. When they look at us, they can praise, approve, critique, judge, condemn, denigrate, shame, or validate us. Conversely, we apply the same judgments to others. We subconsciously detect information based on others' body image. We look at people and evaluate everything about them—their expressions, posture, clothing, tidiness, attitude, etc. These judgments determine how we feel and whether or not we like a person. Likewise, we hold others' opinions of us seriously as we strive for a belonging: approval, popularity, reward—social or otherwise.

We understand that—excluding cameras—only other people's eyes can see our bodies in their entirety as an object/person, which leads them to create a subjective interpretation of what they see. We do the same objective and subjective analyzes when we look at others standing before us. There are hundreds of reasons why it is important to understand what others think of us.

When a client would come to my studio, I had the option to see her or him in different ways: as a person, a human body, a celebrity, an object, a form of advertising, or even an abstract object I'd have to transform with surreal artistry. After I made my choice—or upon the choice of my client—I'd reproduce my idea with the appropriate camera, lighting, and lenses. I'd transfer my subjective interpretation of their object-body into the process of film development or pixels, creating an object that is a photograph. I'd then display that image for anyone to look at, at which point, others would form an opinion on their own interpretation of what they saw in the photo.

A person's interpretation of another individual is based more on their mindset and subjectivity than objective reality. This makes sense because personal history, status, and opinions are part of what categorizes a person as someone you would like or dislike, and it is nearly impossible to like someone who stands for something you morally disagree with. We behave the same way when looking at others. We develop our opinions based on our subjectivity. We value our presentation to others, and we want to portray an accurate image of ourselves so others like us respond with approval and support of our good reputation. Because we can't look upon ourselves directly, we rely on those we admire to validate our opinions and help us form our self-image. We believe these people, we listen to them, and we often do everything in our power to conform to their opinion.

At the same time, we are viewed by everyone we meet: our close friends, our family members, our colleagues, and strangers we pass on the street. We know everyone can draw moral, religious, racial, classist, or otherwise divisive assumptions about us based solely on our appearance. To a certain extent, most of us look and act for others and others look and act for us, constantly mirroring, comparing, matching, competing, associating, and reflecting off one another.

Opinions and predefined ideas—also known as prejudices—affect how we perceive that individual, inevitably resulting in a faulty image. We make assumptions about people. We're likely to assume their facial expressions, actions, and words are created from their making judgments about us. We unconsciously retaliate and make judgments about them. If this is our perspective, we will easily become victims of insecurity and overly sensitive to criticism until we know more about the other person and have a certain closure on their truth.

In the 1990s, neuroscientist Giacomo Rizzolatti and his team at the University of Parma in Italy discovered mirror neurons by observing how newborn monkeys imitate behavior.

MIRROR NEURON

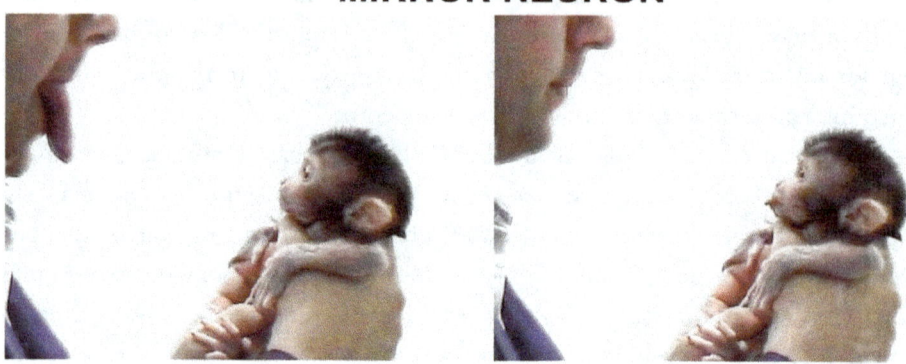

Fig. 1: In the 1990s, Giacomo Rizzolati and his team at the University of Parma in Italy discovered mirror neurons by observing newborn monkeys who easily imitate behavior.
Source: Public Library of Science. Free to distribute under Cc-By-2.5 license.

Mirror neurons activate emotional behavior when the intentions of others are perceived visually. This interaction is innate in us—a survival-oriented biological fact. The discovery of mirror neurons explains how it is natural for us to model, compare, imitate, and learn all sorts of behaviors from others. We see these effects on social media, today. Many people easily attach to trends and mimic the actions of others they see. The results of this behavior on our wellness are still unclear.

We look for happiness and approval from others because we've been conditioned for this ever since we opened our eyes after birth and saw our mothers smiling back at us. We learned everything we knew from the facial expressions and mood of our parents. Our parents would smile if we were good, and they'd frown if we were bad. At a certain point, a frown may proceed with a scolding or punishment. This pattern of judging our success and happiness off facial expressions is all learned behavior. Even when we're grown and capable of independent thought, we continue depending on the opinions of us, because they are a part of us. Every single day, we base our happiness on what we see, hear, and feel from the world around us. We look for happiness outside of ourselves, operating within a system of analysis and reaction to facial expressions and body postures from our friends, spouses, family members, and the rest of society, not to forget the effects of advertising and the images we gather from companies selling their products. Some people spend their lives relying on the approval of others. If they get it, they're happy; if they don't, they lose their way and spiral into misery and depression.

A few years ago, while I was shooting a famous actor for a European magazine, I met his beautiful wife, Carol, and I first noticed her big, kind, beautiful blue eyes. I'd see her again from time to time, at parties or other events, and after a couple of years, she called me for a photo session. She offered a generous sum and, with it, an unusual request: that I turn over the negatives, sell her the copyright, and sign an agreement to never disclose who the shoot was for or what it was about. Intrigued, I accepted the job.

She wanted a set of photos wearing various outfits in different settings with different poses. She wanted to be depicted standing, sitting, lying down, and so on, but peculiarly enough, she only wanted to be photographed with her eyes closed. She requested that no pictures be taken of her with open eyes. And even with her eyes closed, she requested that I photograph her displaying a variety of emotions through different facial expressions. Needless to say, this was one of the strangest photoshoot sessions I've ever experienced. Nevertheless, being a professional, I did what she asked and took my photos of her in all her positions and expressions, but I couldn't help but feel awkward not seeing her eyes. She looked like a sleeping beauty, but recalling the dormant expression her face took on with her eyes closed makes me question how I was ever able to photograph someone like that. It was then that I remembered how I always saw her with her eyes open as wide as they could go, and that she never relaxed them.

After I turned over all of the negatives and printed photos, along with the privacy documents she had me sign, we began to talk about her unusual request to be photographed with closed eyes.

She explained, "Not long ago, I had a couple of my closest friends stay with me as guests while my husband was out of town. It was early one morning, and I was just waking up when I heard my two friends knock at my bedroom door. I was feeling lazy and pretended to be asleep so they wouldn't try to wake me. As they entered, they saw that my eyes were closed and thought I was sleeping. I heard one of them whisper to the other, 'Oh my God! She's ugly. I've never seen her like that.' My other friend replied, 'It's because she's not wearing makeup.' 'No, it's because she really is ugly.' 'She's still asleep. Let's go.' Giggling, they left the room. I was distraught. I was shocked that these people I called my friends could be so rude to me, but I mostly worried that what they were saying was true. I didn't know how to react. I felt paralyzed in my bed after it happened. I did nothing. I went along with them as if nothing had happened, and I merely excused myself by saying I didn't feel good. I never told my husband what happened for fear that a bigger problem would arise, and because I didn't want to look silly. I told my therapist a couple of times but felt little relief. I decided to do a photoshoot because I want to see with my own eyes how ugly I am when my eyes are closed and to know what my friends saw. I carry this in the back of my mind all the time: the doubt as to what I look like and if I am truly ugly to others. I'm afraid of how ridiculous I'd look if others knew how big of a fuss I'm making for some stupid comment."

I didn't know how to respond. This experience showed me how a mere remark by others can destroy your self-image and cause tremendous distortions in your idea of who you are and what you look like. We must let go of what other people think, because, in reality, people form their own subjective opinions of you. If you do not live up to those impressions, it is not your problem; it's their misjudged ideas of who you are. You will feel less concerned with how others see you when you discover your Photo-Image, and you'll be able to accept only the good feedback.

Because you have your Photo-Image in your mind, you can evaluate the exaggerated comments and immediately recognize them as fake. With the Photo-Image, you don't need to overly praise your image or embellish it. You are who you are—no more or less beautiful to yourself than you are to everyone who sees you. This has to be clear in your mind.

Without a proper Photo-Image, our visual link to ourselves is lost. We project our image onto others, making them our personal mirrors, and we become dependent on their reactions toward us. If all we want is to be liked, and if we interpret being liked to mean acceptance, then praise and compliments will give us extreme happiness. Positive feedback will give us intense feelings of self-satisfaction. We'll feel recognized and therefore validated as an entity, which is undoubtedly beautiful and acceptable. The reverse of positive feedback is negative feedback, which triggers the opposite emotions: rejection, fear, inferiority, hopelessness, anger, resentment, and most of all, envy and jealousy, both of which can bloom in hatred. We love the approval of others so much because they represent us as champions of positivity, because we feel positive when other people feel positive about us, even though we may not be generating those feelings from within.

Our need for outside approval results in a never-ending roller coaster ride of acceptance and denial. Being true to yourself means accepting yourself and your reality, whoever you are and whatever it is. Have you ever asked anyone what they would do if they were you? That question boggles my mind. How could someone else know what you should do with your life? Looking to others to tell you how you should look or what you should do will strip you of your energy and identity. Before you know it, you'll find yourself on a path that isn't your own. The further you go down it, the further you'll be from your truth; every step you take, even if you're finding approval from those around you, somehow feels worse. Comparing yourself to others is a never-ending cycle.

As an example, let's take a look at what someone might say if asked to evaluate themselves.

"Here's what I think about myself: Physically, my face is pretty average. I have nice, vivid eyes. Maybe my nose is a little big, but it's alright. My mouth is normal, and overall, I think my face is lovely. My body has some extra pounds on it, but I can fix that anytime. I'm generally healthy, and I look healthy, so that's good. Intellectually, I'm smart, but I need more time to find a way to show my potential. At that point, I'll be able to apply myself seriously. Morally, I think I'm a good person: I have faith in myself, I respect others, and I'm loving. I'm not perfect. I have some problems. I have trouble accepting the injustices in the world. I'm angry about violence. I have problems with people that take what they have for granted. I hate people who lie and gossip, especially those who are fake and talk behind your back. I can't stand when people get rewarded when they don't deserve it and advance their careers just because they know someone. I have my low moments, and, sometimes, I feel inferior to people who look better than I do. I should do more, be more active, and take walks in the morning. I should smile more . . ."

Now let's create a scenario where a friend has a positive opinion of this person.

The friend's opinion is:

"You look marvelous today! I love that color on you. You should wear that more often. It's so nice to see you around. You always make me smile. You're so smart and understanding, and you have great style. I wish I had the willpower that you have. You totally deserve everything you have. You're so well-proportioned and not at all chubby. Don't even think about losing a single pound."

Clearly, this kind of praise would make anyone feel on top of the world. At the very least, you'd gain some confidence that your presence in this world has been noticed. Hearing those words coming from your friend would have you feeling that life is indeed good. You love that friend!

A few days later, the same friend approaches you, and you smile at her with all that love you felt for her the other day. Then, she says:

"What are you smiling about? You look like that bimbo on TV with the weird hair!"

You're stunned. She continues:

"I think chubby people shouldn't wear leggings or colored pants like the ones you always have on. It's so unflattering! It's annoying that I always have to smile back at you, even when I have so many problems. People are always showing off what they have or talking about stupid, superficial stuff. You're embarrassing. I deserve and need a friend who's more interesting, socially advanced, and overall classier than that. By the way, I'm not talking about you or anything. I am just speaking in general terms."

The initial smile on your face transforms into a frown, and you feel pain deep within your heart. This pain will stay with you for as long as you hold this "friend" in high esteem. The pain may never go away, even if at some point, you address your hurt feelings to this person. She may insist that she wasn't talking about you. If you're secure, you'll likely dismiss it and shrug it off as just her opinion. You may even realize she's inconsistent from one meeting to the next and that her reaction has nothing to do with you. Even so, the pain you felt is still there, and you'll feel it when a stranger looks at you in a weird way.

Of course, we don't have to accept people's feedback. We don't *have* to accept any of it—the good or bad—especially when we consider how people can change from one day to the next. Something bad might have happened at work that day, or maybe she got into a fight with her spouse. Maybe that's just how she interacts with "friends." Whatever the case, she said those things to you because she felt bad and needed to transfer those feelings to someone else. Maybe your accepting demeanor gave her the impression that it was okay to behave like that. Most people would never act that way toward an assertive or strong person who might reject that sort of behavior. Most people would never act that way toward someone who has embraced their Photo-Image and knows exactly who they are, and what they will or will not tolerate. This is another reason why having and knowing a Photo-Image is imperative.

We already know that other people may have an image of us that is completely superficial and inaccurate. It is human nature to do this, and there is a good chance we do the same thing to them. We begin to believe that others have power over us that allows them to manipulate our emotional state. What results is a contradiction in which we feel resentment toward people because of their continuous judgment and criticism, while simultaneously, we are compelled to receive criticism in order to be the best overall version of ourselves.

Let go of what other people think of you. They form their own subjective opinions of you. If you don't live up to their misjudged idea of who you are, it's not your problem.

With your Photo-Image in mind, no one else's input is needed for you to know what completes you. You won't need to be overly praised about your image. You won't feel the need to embellish yourself. You will see through exaggerated comments. You will be as beautiful to yourself as you are to everyone else.

4

The Brain's Perception

A HEALTHY BRAIN'S PHYSICAL and biochemical machinery should always be in perfect synchronicity and be able to coordinate all of the functions needed to operate the body. These behaviors are the mental processes that we call the mind.

Developments since René Descartes declared "*I think, therefore I am*" are numerous, but the distinction between our brain and mind still remains a mystery. It is hard to believe that there was doubt about the connection between the brain and the body until only about a century ago. This was because most medical research on the brain focused primarily on brain disease, instead of brain function. Brain research has progressed by huge leaps due to new science and computer technology: mapping the brain, discovering how neurological processes encompass psychological and philosophical aspects of the brain, and the development of thought and personality, establishing a connection between emotions and abilities—creativity, thought, cognition, and movement. So much research goes into understanding just how mental functions—such as perceiving, understanding, thinking, feeling, and decision-making—arise from neural processes in the brain.

In his book *Descartes' Error*, the neurologist Antonio Damasio explained that reasoning depends on a brain system that also processes feelings, and that there is indeed a connection between reason, feeling, and body. The understanding of the human mind requires an organismic perspective; it must be related to a whole organism that consists of body and brain, fully interactive with a physical and social environment.

Damasio wrote, "We are, then we think, and we think only inasmuch as we are, since thinking is indeed caused by the structures and operations of being."

The mind remains an abstract concept. For the purposes of explaining the Photo-Image, I'll use the word *brain* as a whole concept referring to the mind, consciousness, mental processes, and mental activity.

The brain, protected by the cranial cavity, operates undisturbed, according to its natural processes, handling difficult tasks and balancing active work with the other parts of the body. It constantly brings information from the outside world within, processing everything you see, hear, touch, taste, and smell. Each and every day, your brain has to meet the physical and mental needs of your body. The brain completes tasks necessary for the body's optimum functioning subconsciously, and we usually don't think much of it. We are blissfully unaware of the hundred and twenty billion functioning neurons and nerve cells, nor are we attentive to the functions of the cerebral cortex and frontal lobes and their work in maintaining self-control, reasoning, planning, and language. The brain is constantly on, trusting us to give it the right information in order for it to guide us in the right direction.

Let us consider the three distinct pathways of the brain: the neocortex, the limbic brain, and the reptilian brain.

The neocortex is where language is created and ideas and concepts are born. It is also the location for problem-solving, decision-making, and self-regulation. It is the last part of the brain to develop in young adulthood, and it guides behavior with verbal skills and houses the working memory. It is also responsible for the interpretation of facial expressions. It is divided into two hemispheres by the corpus callosum.

The limbic brain—located in the middle of the brain—is a group of forebrain structures including the hypothalamus, amygdala, and hippocampus. These are involved in motivation, emotion, learning, and memory. The autonomic nervous system, the brain's pleasure center, regulates feelings of fear, anger, and joy.

THE BRAIN

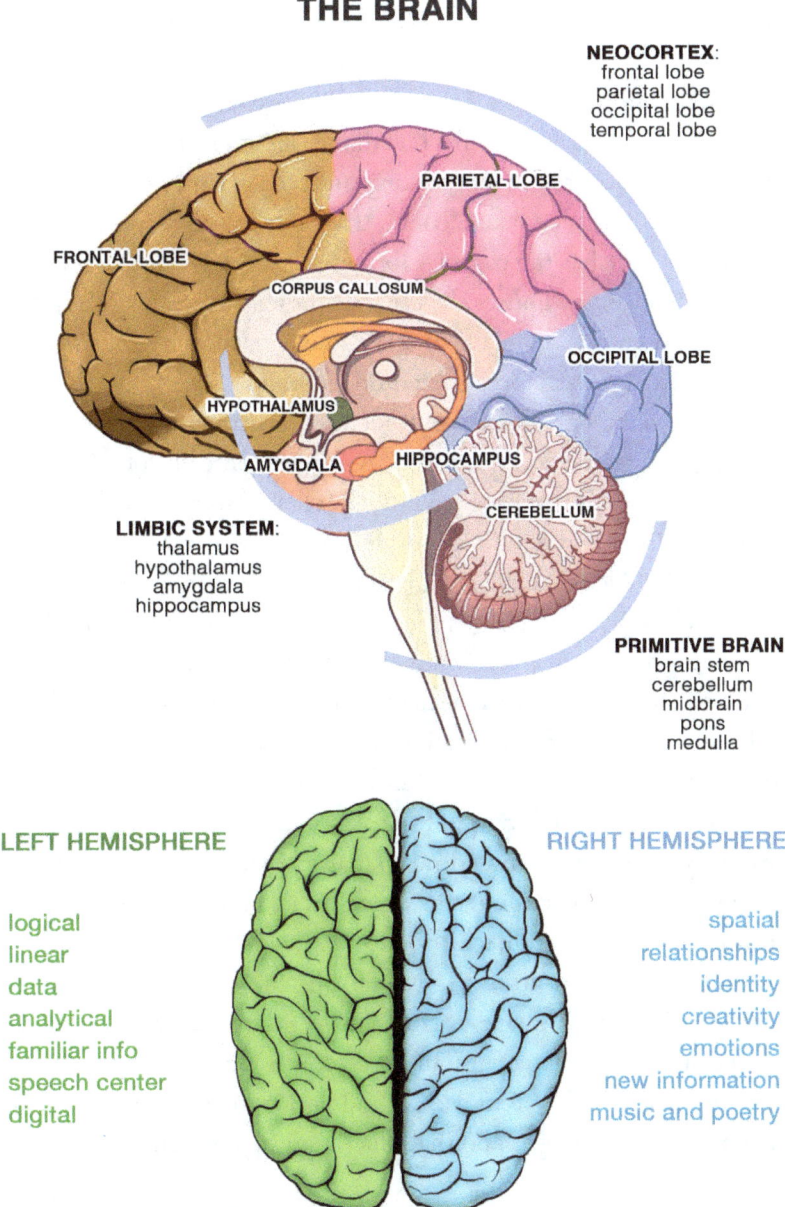

Fig. 2: The different mental functions of the right and left sides
Illustration: Mannig Gurekian

The reptilian—or primitive—brain includes the brain stem, cerebellum, medulla, pons, midbrain, and spinal cord. The primitive brain houses the fight, flight, or freeze defense mechanism. It is the most primitive area of the human brain and maintains basic bodily functions like breathing, digestion, and sleeping. This part of the brain is incapable of conceptualizing time. The primitive brain exists solely to process outside information and control the body's response to the senses.

Each hemisphere has the capacity for unique cognitive processing. For most of us, the left hemisphere houses the capacity for logical and analytical thinking, the ability to retain facts and data, and is also where speech centers are located. The right hemisphere processes spatial information. The ability to understand concepts, metaphors, and the sense of identity is also found here, where emotionally triggered memories are stored. A speech center is located in the right hemisphere that applies language from the left hemisphere to produce meaningful phrases—this is how poetic language can be both created and understood. The long-standing idea that the right brain is the more emotional is true in this respect, as it controls the feelings of fear, mourning, and overall pessimism.

Connecting the hemispheres and their respective capacities is the corpus callosum—the largest structure in the brain—which is a network of fibers that bridge the hemispheres and facilitate function in harmony. It unites the special functions of each hemisphere, combining the left side's logical, linear mode of thinking and the right side's concept of relationship and identity.

Obviously, it is our brain and not our eyes that form images in our head. That is why we often hear the terms *mental image* and *mental imagery,* referring to a memory or an eidetic image that forms in the back of our brain—in the visual cortex—and stores itself in our subconscious mind. That said, the eyes are crucial in the brain's image creation process. In the eye, the light rays go through the surface of the cornea and create a refracted light ray. Take a look at how the human visual system works, and notice the similarities between the physical structure of the eyes and that of a photographic camera.

How the Brain Perceives the Body

A groundbreaking researcher in the neurosurgery field was Wilder Penfield (1891–1976), who dedicated his life to the research of human understanding while attempting to find the cure to acute epilepsy. He would operate on conscious patients under local anesthesia to observe their responses, and use those to target the precise areas of the brain responsible for epilepsy. This technique allowed him to discover new information about brain function regarding how stimulating certain parts of the cerebral cortex provoked reactions in other areas, such as memory, sound, and movement. He found associations between various limbs and organs, the sensory and motor cortex, and lateralization of brain functions.

Penfield created an imaginary character based on his discoveries on the motor cortex, and his brain maps showed which areas were activated in reference to body parts. The character—the homunculus—resembled a cartoon-like figure that illustrates the comparative brain space activated by the body's organs and muscles. Essentially, the homunculus is a visual representation of the brain's perception of its motor activity of parts of the body based on their activity, number of sensory nerves, and size. Penfield's homunculus shows a complete example of the differences between our brain's interpretation of our body parts within our field of view as opposed to those outside it.

THE HOMUNCULUS

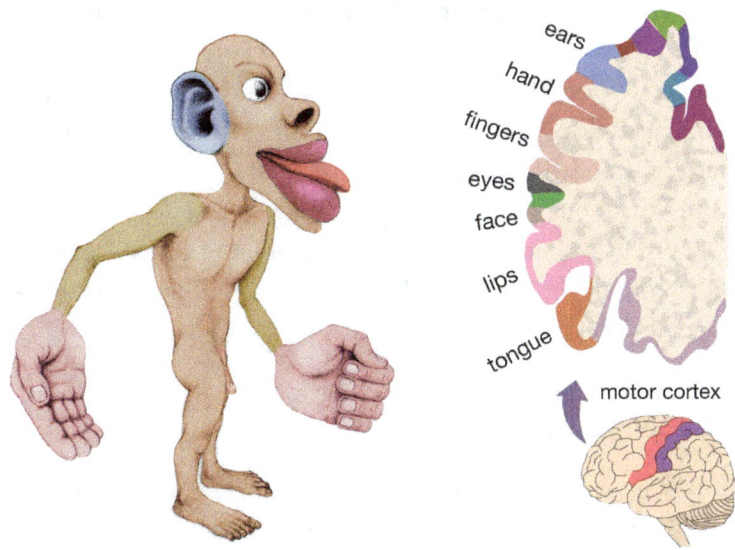

Fig. 3: The homunculus is an imagined caricature of how bodily activity is perceived by the motor cortex
Illustration: Paola Barcaccia

Let us use some examples. The mouth is just outside of your field of view, so your brain doesn't have a clear visual image of it, but it has a pretty good idea about what's going on. You know this because you constantly feel your mouth, and you almost always know your mouth's muscle activity, vocal activity, sense of taste, and salivation. The brain has a pretty good understanding of the mouth for the enormous activity in which it engages. In the homunculus, the mouth is depicted as being huge because the brain is constantly aware of it. Your feet often perform right on the edge of your field of vision as well during walking, climbing, and kicking, but your brain is constantly aware of them. As for the genitals, you can achieve a greater sense of stimulation when you see them. When you form a visual connection with a body part, you are able to achieve a greater sense of feeling and control.

On the other hand, your hands are almost always in your field of view because they are right in front of your eyes. This added visualization aids in your brain's overall understanding and performance of your hands. This is necessary as they are often used to complete minute and delicate actions. Consider for a moment the magnitude of humanity's advancements stemming from the creative use of our hands and the importance of our long opposable thumbs, dexterous fingers, and the ability to rotate our wrist.

The importance of this becomes clear when we recognize that our knowledge of an object changes our perception of it. We can see everything in the world except our body image, visually or mentally.

Knowing that your brain senses your body—despite limited visual information—in order to acquire a solid representation of internal and external organs based on motor activity and other various cues is critical in understanding how to approach seeing your body.

The Visual Process

The eyeball is an organ with specialized neural tissue and includes the lens and the cornea—a clear surface that covers the front of the eye and protects it while refracting light rays as they enter the eye. The light continues through the pupil, the iris, and the lens to bring an object into a focus inside your head. The lens has two important functions: adjusting its curvature (based on an object's distance) to refract light rays and inverting the image into the retina. The retina, located at the back of the eye, is laden with neuron circuits and transmitters for the brain. It contains photoreceptors—rods and cones—that detect light and connect with the central nervous system. Their function is to absorb wavelengths of light and convert them into electrical signals that are sent through the optic nerves to the optic chiasm of the brain.

In the optic chiasm, each picture is divided in half. The outer half of each picture continues to the visual cortex. The inner halves cross over to the other side of the brain first and then continue to the visual cortex, where the visual information from each eye is processed, combined, and converted into what we call sight.

In photography, light rays from an object pass through a camera lens where concave and convex lenses adjust for distance and focus, just like the cornea and lens function in the eye. As with vision, light rays have to refract to a point where an inverted image is created, just like in the visual cortex of the brain. Unlike the eye, most cameras have mirrors that reflect the image to the viewfinder in order for the image to be viewed correctly. Still, cameras do, in fact, register images upside down first, just like the visual cortex in the brain.

In terms of your Photo-Image, cameras are the only appropriate substitute for the eyes, as they have the same structure, the same precision, and can be just as detailed in their perception of the image as the brain.

The brain sees everything within our field of vision from the neck down as a partial version of its real image: our bodies, especially our hands, feet, genitals, or breasts. All other features seen by the brain are only partially observed, resulting in an unclear visual image. Images are reversed and in an inverted position in the occipital visual cortex.

Understanding the physical structure of the visual system is paramount to understanding why our visual interpretation of our own body parts will always be limited. Understanding our eyes allows us to face the simple reality that we just can't see anything that's outside of our field of vision. Therefore, it's impossible for us to see our own eyes, ears, mouth, most of our nose, and the general entirety of our face.

VISUAL PATHWAYS

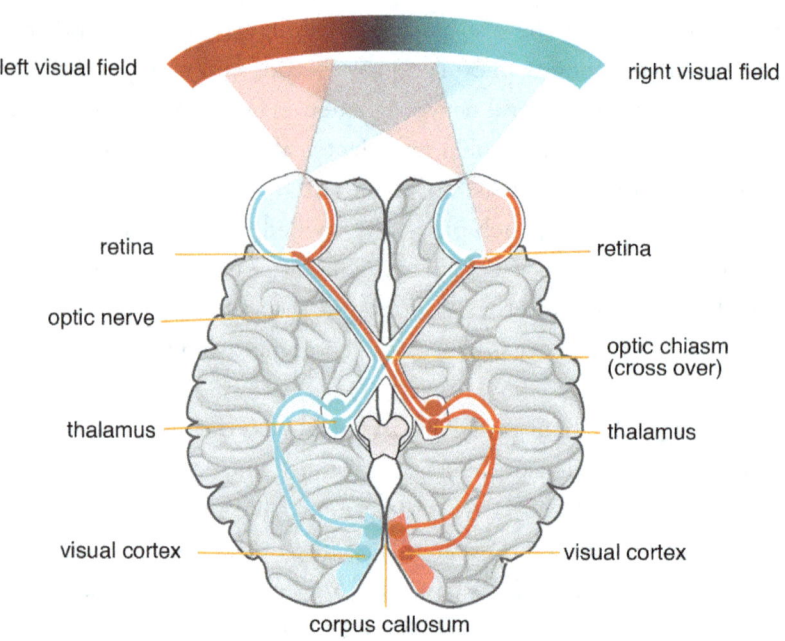

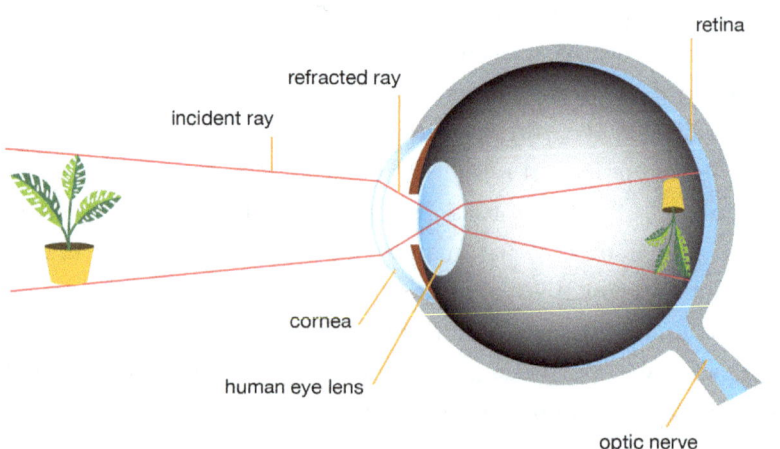

Fig. 4a: The visual pathways. How images reach the visual cortex of the
Illustration: Mannig Gurekian

SIMILARITY BETWEEN CAMERA AND EYE

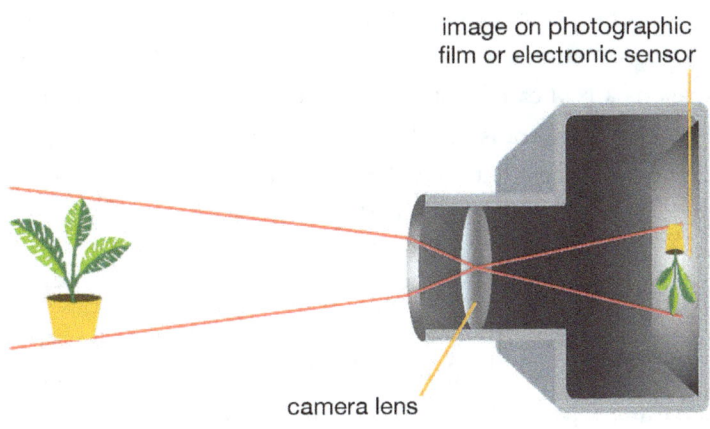

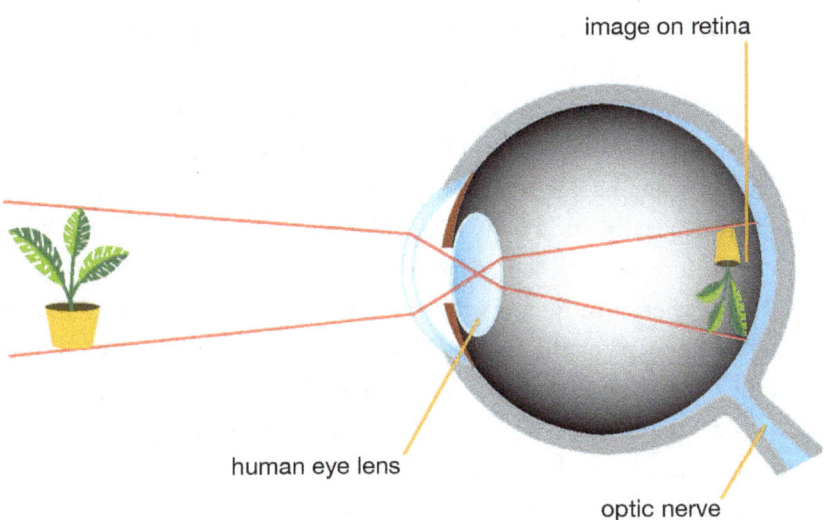

Fig. 4b: The physical structure of the eyes and how they perceive images is very similar to that of the camera.
Illustration: Mannig Gurekian

How Images Are Created

Our eyes and cameras are the only two mechanisms in existence that can create images. Objects can only be seen when illuminated, and only become images when they are interpreted by eye or by a camera. The object becomes an image, and the image is a replica of that object as it is: all qualities, meaning, or values of the object itself are transferred into the image. To be clear, if an image doesn't contain the attributes that come from that object, it will be the image of another object. Therefore, an image is the result of a totality of an object. Images and objects are one.

Everything existing in nature or manufactured, whether animate or inanimate, is considered an object. An object is defined by irregular rays reflecting from its form. The object has to be defined also by a physical entity. Matter has attributes such as dimensions and color, and, if animated, by motion in time and space. This information is conveyed to the eyes, which prepare an image of the object to be sent by the rods and cones through the optic chiasm to be perceived by the visual cortex located in the back of the brain.

Your eyes transfer a subjective image to your brain, and your brain responds with as reasonable a reaction as it possibly can. The brain is not responding to the object itself, but instead to your sensory and emotional history of the image you perceive. Your interpretation of an object stems from your knowledge of that object and the concepts and abstract ideas you associate with it. Of course, this also factors heavily into how we see other people; we see everybody differently and therefore react to each person uniquely and subjectively.

We then experience feelings that we project onto the images and create a meaning or concept of the object. Images are interconnected with our five senses—they are always accompanied by sensations and are often linked with words, music, etc. and tied with emotions. There are no images without emotions, and no emotions without images. This is the universal structure of understanding objects and our relation to them.

Again, an image doesn't exist without the eye's vision to interpret it, nor can an image exist without being a reflection of an object and something perceptible by the senses. The duty of the senses is to transport information from the outside world to the brain to give meaning to the object-image. Your brain's image will be a subjective idea or conceptualization and interpretation of that object. Images formed in the brain must be congruent with the other senses, including the sound, touch, smell, and taste of the object. The image of an object cannot exist in your brain without an initial idea, concept, or knowledge of that object. Therefore, there cannot be an image without a subjective interpretation of that object. In the same way, there cannot be an image without emotions or feelings attached to it.

For example, if you see a tree, you take note of details like its size, color, and leaf shape. The tree's identity becomes increasingly real as you sense it and your knowledge of it expands. The more you know, the more you build on the concept or idea of that tree. With that concept come feelings—both pleasurable and non-pleasurable. Sensations and feelings are elicited when you associate and compare these images with other past images of trees you have seen. If you are a tree expert and already know everything there is to know about the tree, you will have different feelings toward it then someone who only knows basic facts about the tree and would not be able to tell the difference between it and any other kind of tree. The same can be said about a magician watching a magic show. They'll probably be less amused than you if you aren't a magician yourself. Conversely, they may be more amused at the same time, because they understand the difficulty of the trick. The more you know about an object, the easier it is for your brain to make an accurate evaluation and a confident response to that image.

Though the brain can see everything in front of its eyes, it fails when it comes to seeing its body. It lacks a precise image of what exactly it is protecting, balancing, coordinating, analyzing, acknowledging, and beautifying. Our bodies are physical objects with physical properties, and if I do not see my body as an object in front of my eyes, I cannot have an image of my body-self. And if I do not have an image of myself, I don't have the precise knowledge of who I am the same way I make sense of everyone and everything I see in the world.

It is impossible to know ourselves without knowing our image. You cannot know the characteristics and qualities of an image that you cannot see entirely. Aside from what the brain knows, sees, hears, or understands, the brain cannot see our facial expressions nor our physical proportions. If it cannot operate consistently, it becomes confused about who you are. This confusion leads to feelings of anxiety, identity issues, and an unclear understanding of what we want.

The brain also stores emotional mental images from our past that keep us from objectively processing our present experiences. Take a minute to remember an image or photo of yourself. Whatever you see will come with the attached feelings from that moment in time. You can only see that image with past emotions, not the emotions you feel today. As you recall the past, you recall the emotions as well. The way we constantly reenact the pain or joy of the past makes it difficult to let it go. It is also why changes can be so difficult. Not only that, it is nearly impossible for your mind to recall an episode of your life without emotion.

Despite that, a photograph is still the only mechanism apart from our eyes that can objectively capture an image. The distinct advantage a camera has over all other media of image creation is that it has all of the same physical structures as the human eye. Painters, sculptors, and other artists must rely not only on their eyes but their hands to attempt to produce an image. The problem with those forms of image creation is that it depends too heavily on subjective interpretation: often, subjectivity is the goal in fine art, as it is used to communicate a feeling more than a perfect representation of what is real. Like the human eye and the visual cortex, which see and create both images and mental images, the camera can also see, create, and retain images on film, paper, and pixel. The invention of the camera was a major innovation in the nineteenth century, and it completely changed the way we live our lives.

The inventor of photography, Joseph Nicéphore Niépce, produced the first photograph in 1826, titled *The View from the Window at Le Gras.*

THE FIRST PHOTOGRAPH

Fig.5: In 1826, Nicéphore Niépce produced the first photograph titled *The View from the Window at Le Gras.*

Niépce's "heliograph" was created by coating a piece of metal with naturally occurring asphalt called Bitumen of Judea. Bitumen hardens when exposed to light. The first photograph, *The View from the Window at Le Gras,* was a complicated process that took eight hours to expose. Louis Jacques Daguerre eventually took possession of Niépce's heliotype, improved it substantially, and reduced the exposure time from four hours to one minute. He considered the improved technique his own invention and named his pictures Daguerreotypes. The Daguerreotype was an instant success in Europe and especially in America upon its release, which brought popularity to Louis Daguerre, while Niépce's name slowly faded away, only mentioned marginally in some books.

William Henry Fox Talbot, an English mathematician and scientist, created a different method to Daguerre's, placing light-sensitive chemicals on paper and aiming light through a box. The image that was exposed on the paper was a negative—all of the light in the picture was dark and vice versa. His experiments had begun in early 1834. This process made him the true creator of the negative and positive photographic process. The ability to create multiple prints from a single negative is what sets Talbot's process apart from Daguerre's, which could only make a single image from a single exposure.

Photography exposed the beauty of the world. It helped people experience foreign cultures and faraway lands without having to go anywhere far, and it allowed the common person to study their own image like never before. However, until now, photography wasn't able to capture the entirety of a being. A Photo-Image created through a photographer is the only true way to transform an individual into an object that can subsequently be seen as an image of the self from which it stems.

When we see other people in front of us, we see them with a clarity that we lack in the image we have of ourselves, unless we have a Photo-Image. That missing information leaves us feeling unhappy and incomplete. Even those who allegedly have it all can end up being confused, because their idea of self is blurry. A client I had struggled with this for many years.

Her story is a perfect example of how misleading the mirror image is, and how easily tricked our brains can be. In her particular case, her brain was unable to adjust after a plastic surgery, which caused her to fail to see the results of the surgery, despite what the mirror was showing her.

This client was American, but I had previously done a few photoshoots with her for European magazines. She was funny, friendly, and very beautiful. Unlike other celebrities, who usually wanted to choose their favorite pictures at the end of the shoot, she preferred that I make that choice for her. "I trust you. Whatever you chose for me is good," she would say, jokingly. "You know I'm photogenic!"

This young woman always brought me a certain type of confidence when we were shooting. She would arrive with a huge smile on her face and always light up the whole studio. This time was very different, though. As soon as she came in, she apologized for not having her makeup done.

"I'm sorry, Pina, I barely slept after last night. I didn't want to cancel on you, but I also didn't want to stay home. I just don't feel like shooting today."

I told her not to worry. If she didn't feel good, the photos would show it. We didn't have to continue the photoshoot. I told her to sit down with me and asked her if she wanted to talk about what had happened.

She stared at me for a few seconds.

"Last night was a nightmare. I went to a friend's birthday party, and it was fun at first. You know, the house was packed, the food was great . . . but when we were singing happy birthday, I noticed that there was a woman staring intensely at me from across the room. As soon as our eyes met, she screamed 'It's you! Oh my God, it's you,' and ran over to hug me. I smiled and embraced her as I started to recognize who she was: a middle school friend who I hadn't seen in over eighteen years. She continued, loudly, 'I was looking at you all night long, but I couldn't remember how I knew you! Then, when our eyes met, I knew it was you! It's impossible to recognize you! What happened to your brown hair, your braces, and your huge nose?'

"She kept going, 'I love the color of your hair! Honestly, I'm glad that you got rid of that elephant trunk.' At that moment, everyone turned and looked at us, then me, then at my nose. I almost passed out. She laughed, and so did some other people. I whispered, 'Can you be a little bit more discreet; what is wrong with you?' She responded, 'Sorry, I couldn't help it when I recognized you. I was so happy to see you as this beautiful star you are now!' I snapped, 'Shut up! This is none of your business!' and I stormed away. On my way out, I could hear people chattering, and I felt humiliated. I knew that I was going to be the talk of the night."

She was silent for a moment, holding back tears.

"So, that was my evening! After I got home, I couldn't fall asleep and just cried helplessly into the morning. I didn't feel like seeing anyone, but I had to leave my house."

I held her hand and told her not to be too hard on herself.

"Nobody cares what people at a party talk about. Honestly, so what if someone did notice it? If they ask you, just answer candidly that you had a little nose touch up. It's no big deal. Almost everyone in this industry has had work done. Some have had so much Botox pumped into their face that they look like Donald Duck."

She let out a deep breath and said, "If you saw my photograph when I was fifteen, you would not recognize me. You know, this nightmare actually started in elementary school. Kids constantly picked on me for my ugly brace face and my huge nose. Whenever I sneezed, they all made elephant noises. They nicknamed me 'Ele,' short for Elephant. I always tried to be quiet and friendly to everyone, but the nicer I was to them, the more they picked on me. At the age of fourteen, I told my parents I wanted to get a nose job. Their reaction was, categorically, 'No.' Little by little, they began to understand. They saw how I was bullied every day and the emotional problems that it was causing me. My father scheduled a consultation with a specialist at the end of the school year. I had to have two surgeries done, due to how large the bones between my eyes were. The surgery was incredibly painful, but I didn't care. I was just finally happy.

"Sixteen and seventeen were the best years of my life. I had many friends and was very popular. I even forgot about how I used to look. But, soon after, I started to act strange. I changed my hair color at least once a week and dressed in over-the-top outfits. I fought with my mother constantly. I was being extremely rebellious. Then, one day out of nowhere, I looked at the mirror and saw 'Ele' again, and that was the start of my downfall. I knew I was beautiful now, but I constantly imagined people making fun of me, of 'Ele' and her big nose.

"It was like I was two different people. One beautiful and happy, especially when I was on set and in front of a camera, and the other sad and ugly as hell, when I was anywhere else. When I started working, I needed to go to a therapist, and she has given me comfort and help for the past ten years. But today, like last night," she said, as her eyes fill up with tears again, "I see myself as 'Ele,' with clear, vivid pictures in my mind, it's as if I was that middle school girl again."

She took a deep breath.

"But don't feel bad for me. These feelings pass . . ."

She left the studio after our conversation. A few days later, she called me and asked me to go over to her house. She called because she wanted to show me a picture of her as a teenager, as 'Ele.' As soon as she handed me the photo, we looked at each other and started laughing uncontrollably. We couldn't stop.

"You know, I really was 'Ele,'" she said, looking at the picture.

At least she was able to laugh at herself, too. Once we calmed down, I started explaining my process of Photo-Image to her. She was intrigued and booked a session.

I SEE MYSELF, THEREFORE I AM

I was hesitant while I took her photos. Did she understand what Photo-Image was all about? She was used to having her photos taken, but they were usually glamorous, stylish photoshoots. Photo-Image isn't like that. It is a very simple photo that reflects the true person behind the subject's face. It is not about what you look like, it is about who you are. Only when you are true to yourself will you be truly comfortable with what you look like. This understanding is necessary to achieve a higher level of confidence in yourself and your beauty. Once "Ele" grasped this concept, she was able to see her true beauty. She eventually became one of my best friends and promoters.

The Photo-Image was particularly helpful to "Ele" because, as we know, the laws of physics state an object must be visible to our eyes in order for our brains to comprehend it. Only then can the brain create an accurate image of that object. Afterward, the brain freely incorporates and integrates that photographic information with all its sensory information. Only once everything is integrated can a fully functioning brain trust that it has a true self-image to reference. This is like the completion of an elaborate work of art visible in your brain as a real object in the world.

This is something we need to feel complete and secure in knowing who we are and what we look like. By integrating our visual self with our brain, we feel whole. When the brain sees an image—Photo-Image—that it registers as a true image of your face and body, it can make an evaluation and form a complete concept of yourself. At that point, knowledge of yourself begins to fuel your self-image with concrete information. You will find that you focus more on yourself and feel a reinvigorated desire to surround yourself with the things and people you care about the most. You will be led to a greater understanding of your potential, and your wild creativity will find direction as mental processes expand. Your brain will pull you in the direction that will be best for you. With your brain functioning at its maximum mental wholeness, you will begin to feel an intrinsic responsibility for your own well-being and a call to give yourself the best you can have.

Only with your Photo-Image will your brain find its direction. By keeping it in front of you, your mind's eye will become your internal North Star. With a glance, you will be able to reaffirm your sense of self and find personal assurances that the path you are on is correct, instead of an ambiguous gray area when it comes to career, goals, and love.

    Simply having your own image in front of you will give you strength through your awareness of your presence in time and space. It will serve as a constant reminder of your potential, guiding actions from within, unaffected by the pressure from forces without.

5

The Virtual Image in the Mirror

IT MAKES SENSE to base your knowledge of yourself on the mirror's reflection. Despite this, by now we all know mirrors are neither adequate nor accurate as a visual tool for us to determine deeper truths about our image.

There are many reasons why it is more difficult for people to know how they look in a mirror than a photo or video, including:

- You're used to the reflection in the mirror.
- The lateralization of your face flips.
- You have a defensive, yet unconscious idea of how other people see you.
- You have a different image of yourself in your mind's eye.
- Someone told you or you're convinced you're unattractive.
- You don't know what to look for in your face

The physics of the mirror is a must-know in order to understand why we are unable to see ourselves. This problem is both psychological and physical, and truly understanding the issue will help us fix it. That is why it is important to take a close look at the basic composition of mirrors and the physics behind them.

A plane (flat) mirror is often made of glass over a layer of silver nitrate or aluminum reflecting solution, covered with a coat of paint that protects the reflective stratum from scratching.

The law of reflection says a plane mirror reflects incident light rays at an equal angle of incidence, as indicated in Figure 6.

What you see in the mirror is a virtual image. The virtual image is a perceived replica of an object, and it is formed when your line of sight goes directly to the image location and light from the object reflects off the mirror. You will see the incident ray reflecting back from the mirror's surface without passing through the image point. This means you are only able to see your image at that exact point where your eyes look. Therefore, the virtual image is backward.

The law of reflection says that a virtual image forms behind the range of the incident ray and the reflected ray, meaning the virtual image does not reflect light in itself. This is the major difference between it and the real image. Bear in mind that the only things that produce light are the sun, stars, fire, and electricity, and that every other object we see is made visible by the light reflected by these sources onto the object.

To visualize this, think of the moon—a dark object, devoid of light, yet, because of its position in space, rough surface, and physical composition, it is able to reflect sunlight and become the illuminated object we see at night. Depending on its position in space, sun rays reflect in different directions. The more the reflection, the closer the moon is to being full. In physics, this is called diffused reflection.

LAW OF REFLECTION

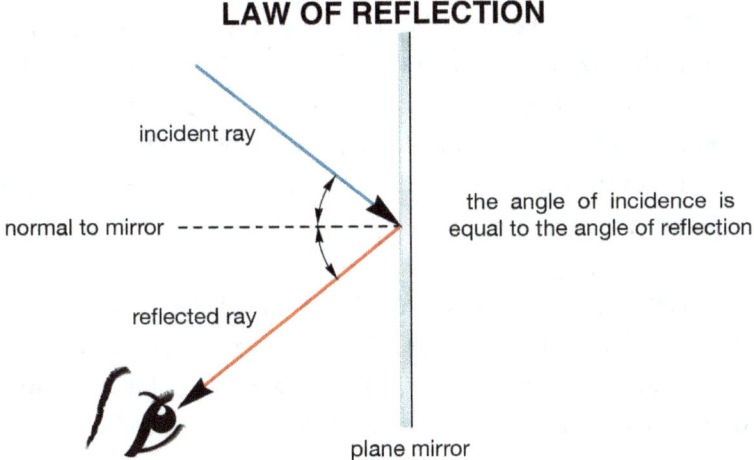

Fig. 6: The law of reflection is applied to plane mirrors or any other reflecting surface.

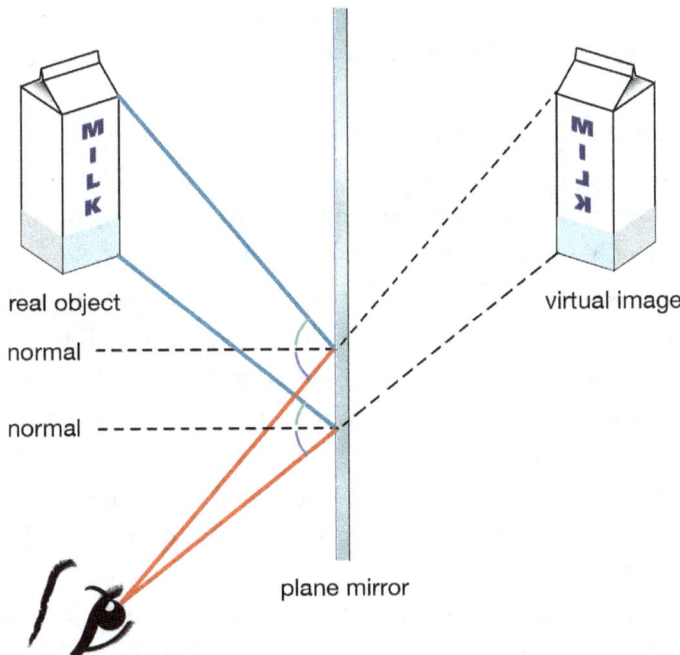

Fig. 6: The virtual image does not exist in reality.
Illustration: Mannig Gurekian

The difference between an object that reflects light and an object that doesn't is how they are recognized by the brain. The non-reflective virtual image in the mirror is an inaccurate illusion of a real image, and your brain understands that, whether you like it or not. The virtual image from the mirror can reach the retina of the eyes as a registered illusion, but since the image does not project light rays, it cannot reach the visual cortex where the image is formed in the brain.

Even though most people base their image on what they see in the mirror, they do not consider the reflection as a virtual image. You recognize yourself in the mirror because you are conscious of standing in front of it. The image in the mirror only exists as long as you see it and only until it is acknowledged by your brain, your mind, and your senses. Only through reasoning do you recognize that the mirror image is, in fact, you. Notice how you can only examine one feature of yourself at a time when you observe your face, and that you cannot pay attention to your face as a whole. Your attention span seems short as your eyes hover over each point on your face, unable to focus on one spot for too long. Why?

To find this answer, I experimented by asking my subjects to describe or draw their image after an extended look in a mirror. Even after staring for minutes, most were completely unable to describe anything but a vague image. Some could only remember the sensation in their bodies. Some remembered the color of their clothes because they observed them directly with their own eyes, avoiding the mirror entirely. Furthermore, when I prodded my subjects to try to describe their features in any way, they were all able to draw in detail from a past photograph or video they remembered but were unable to gather anything from their recent look into the mirror.

The virtual image in the mirror is backward. Your right and left sides are reversed. The brain interprets this image as backward from the function of its left and right hemispheres.

As Figure 7 explains, each side of your brain controls the opposite side of your body. These hemispheres dictate how our body functions.

BRAIN AND VIRTUAL IMAGE

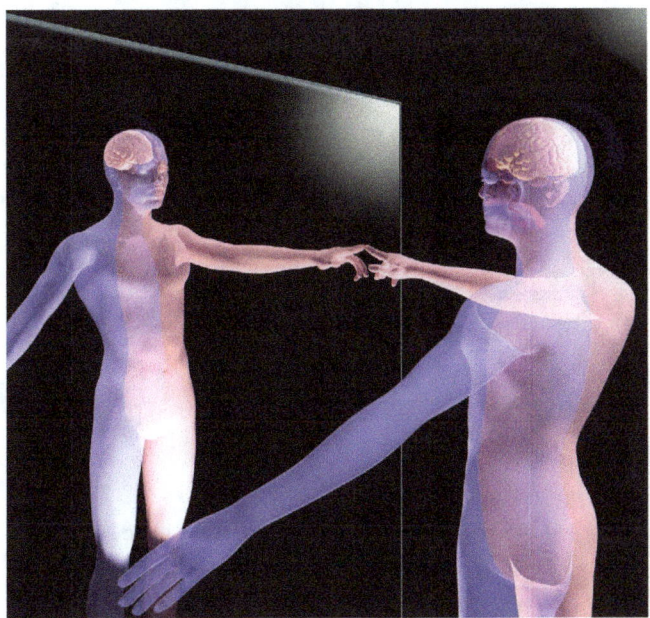

Fig. 7: The right side of the brain controls the left side of the body and vice versa. In the plane mirror, we perceive our right side as our left and our left side as our right.

Illustration: Riccardo Mazzucco

The functions of each hemisphere are vital for the brain to process sensory information. The brain cannot afford to make mistakes. Simple as it sounds, the ability to make precise motor functions relies on the correct analysis of what is right and left, and the brain cannot afford to be misrepresented or fooled by what it may assume to know. For example, your left hemisphere is activated when you use your right hand to brush your hair. Your brain carefully registers the positions of your body parts and manipulates your movements according to your desired outcome. In Figure 8, when brushing in front of the mirror, it will appear that the left hand is moving when it is simply a reflection. How can the brain confidently relate to a flipped image while the right motor area is activated in moving the arm if its reference image is reversed?

RIGHT HAND VS LEFT HAND

Normal photo with brush in right hand.

Photo in the mirror with brush in left hand.
Fig. 8: Right hand vs left hand.

When you look at your face in the mirror, you don't see yourself the way anyone else does. Your right and left face are slightly different from each other due to the lateralization of the face caused by the two hemispheres responsible for facial symmetry. If you think your right side looks better than your left when you are looking in the mirror, it is actually your left side that looks better in real life. This is part of the reason people get confused when they see photos of themselves and say, "This isn't me!" or "I don't look good in photos." In reality, they are comparing what they see in a photo to what they see in a mirror. They are familiar with their mirror image, so they assume that is what they look like. It's not! Your real image—what you look like and how others see you—is what you look like in a photograph.

fMRI (functional magnetic resonance imaging) research has shown that much of the brain's image of their person is formed by perception, tactile sensation, kinesthetic feeling, and self-thought that occurs every time it interacts with a mirror image. An image will almost always look better to a person when they are happy than when they are depressed, and a happy person will almost always think they are beautiful while a depressed person is more likely to consider themselves ugly. We subject ourselves to these varying, mood-based interpretations of our image every time we look in the mirror.

Much of the reason we suffer self-doubt and anxiety is the confusing and fickle way our brain attempts to make sense of our reality. Because we are unable to see ourselves in a true manner, we create space for confusion and anxiety to grow. The problem again roots itself on our inaccessibility to a true understanding of ourselves. The vision you have of your entire body in a mirror, on the other hand, is generally vague and a result of the combination of both sensation and perception. This is why, we can never truly know who we really are, despite looking in a mirror several times daily. To be able to see your body in its entirety, you should have a mirror one and one-half times your height.

The mirror image is merely a hint or glimpse of your own image and not an exact representation. Your image should not be dependent on a mirror's reflection, especially since self-perception plays such a big role in determining the outcome of what we see. This is also why your mind cannot picture you as a self-image. No image is registered in your brain based on what you see in the mirror. Don't reject who you perceive yourself as being, especially when your mood is not positive. This does not mean you should not look in the mirror. Just, be aware and use the image in the mirror only as a suggestion or a tool for dressing, styling, and applying makeup, but not as a window to view yourself with judgment.

THE TRUTH OF THE FACE

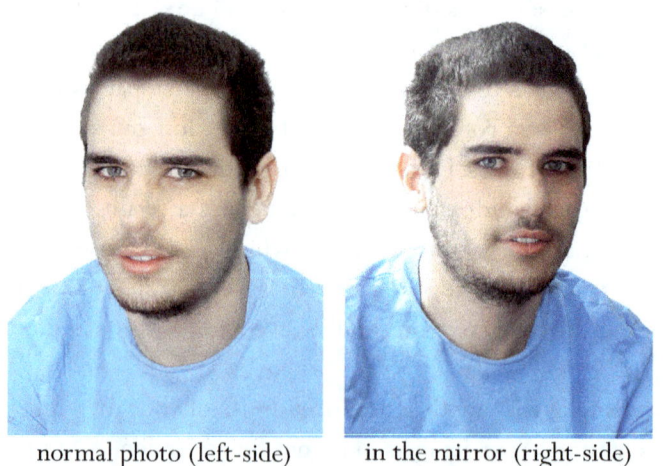

normal photo (right-side)   in the mirror (left-side)

Fig. 9: From left to right—the real image and the reflected image in the mirror.

normal photo (left-side)   in the mirror (right-side)

Fig. 10: From left to right—the real image and the reflected image in the mirror.

Notice the difference in shape and size.

Figure 9, 10: The mirror image functions as a photoshopped image. It is soft and diffused, in contrast to the more detailed and precise photographic image. Of course, we prefer the mirror image compared to the photo.

Lateralization

Do you know what is the best side of your face? To further complicate this complexity, we need to take into consideration the lateralization of the face.

You have probably noticed that the right and left sides of your face are slightly different from each other due to the lateralization of the face caused by the two hemispheres responsible for facial symmetry. People always ask to have a picture taken of their best side—which they usually have backward because they are used to their mirror image—or they ask me which side is better.

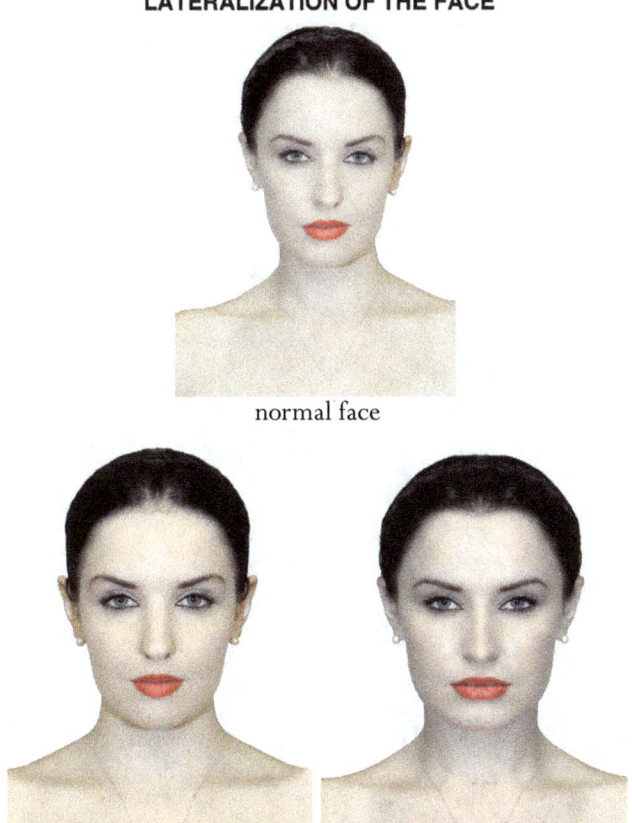

Fig. 11: The asymmetry of faces reflecting the differences in shape and character.

Facial lateralization, or laterality, refers to the right and left hemispheres of the brain, and their different functions evidenced by their asymmetry, size, measure, and function. The two sides have a reflecting effect on the face and, of course, on facial expression. Each side of the brain corresponds to the opposite side of the face. For example, a left-hemisphere-dominant brain will refer to the right side of the face and vice versa. When you compare your face in a mirror and in a photograph, the difference becomes evident. This photo shows the asymmetry of faces related to the two brain hemispheres, reflecting the difference in shape and character.

LATERALIZATION OF THE FACE

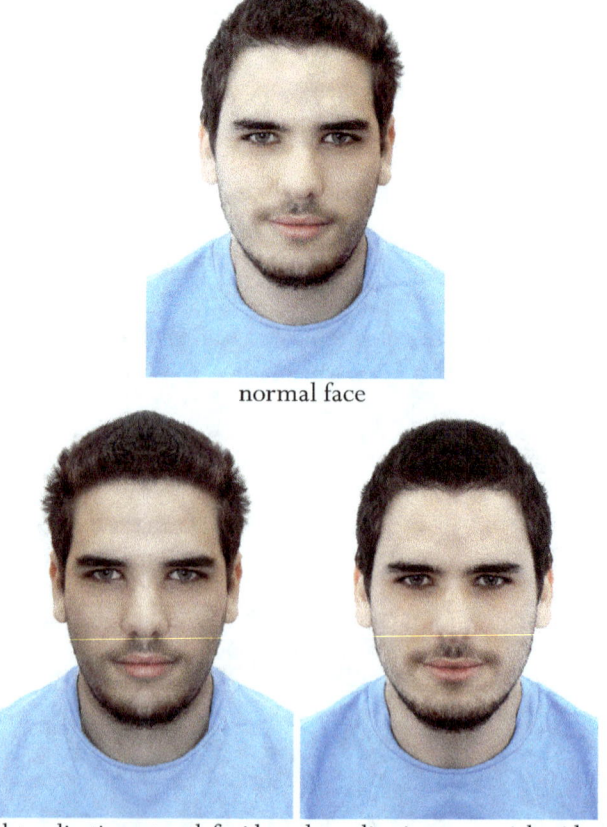

normal face

lateralization - two left sides   lateralization - two right sides

Fig. 12: The asymmetry of faces reflecting the differences in shape and character.

I SEE MYSELF, THEREFORE I AM

Facial laterality affects a person's point of view, confidence, and beauty. In women, I have found the left side is often softer and more expressive than the right. For men, the right side emphasizes a more masculine attitude and character. Knowing this fact is not only convenient for having your picture taken but also in finding confidence in communication, meetings, or important interviews to assure you look your best and show your full personality.

This is the reason why you might be confused when you see yourself in a photo. You are comparing what you see in a mirror to what you see in a photograph. You are used to looking in the mirror, so you assume that is what you look like. The real you is how others see you and what you look like in a photograph. Even though photographs, on the whole, are the most accurate way to capture your image, most photographs still capture a false—or rather, misleading—image of yourself.

Our brains constantly need to see something in order to be able to compare ourselves to something. Because we cannot have our body object-image in front of us, we look to other people in order to form an image of what we look like in our minds. Our brains accept all comparisons, imitations, and visual information it receives from others, both objective and subjective, no matter how confusing it may be. This is further proof that the brain cannot access the visual information it needs from the mirror alone. You stand in front of the mirror for hours, impeccably dressed, looking like the most beautiful version of yourself you have ever seen and still lack conviction in what you see in the mirror. We try to escape this confusion by either conforming to or challenging the rules of others, fueled by our need for others' approval to help our brain match its mental image with the image we have of ourselves.

Imagine a bride preparing for her wedding day. She has taken months getting ready, but no matter what she looks like in the mirror, the only impression that counts occurs the moment she reveals herself in public. Upon stepping before the waiting eyes of the crowd, she will immediately look for positive reinforcement to confirm her beliefs about how she looks. Only then can she truly say, "I look beautiful." She will continue seeking affirmations throughout the wedding: confirmation of her love from her groom, confirmation of excitement through the crowd, and repeated confirmations of her beauty from her guests. Even after the wedding, the bride will continue to seek confirmation and self-reinforcement through wedding photographs. Nobody, not even her new husband, can convince her of her beauty more than her own opinion of the photos in her wedding album. Only a photograph can give her the true image of what she looked like on that special day.

Seeing Someone Else in the Mirror

There is another thing to take into consideration. When we are in front of a mirror, we dissociate ourselves from the person we see. We see an image of us that we recognize as ourselves—we see our face and our body, but that image is not us. It is a virtual image, or a false illusion. We then think about that person's reflection, it is not *me* I see, but *her*. While doing this, we unconsciously impersonate somebody who has a big influence on us, either negative or positive.

My friend Francesca often comes to LA for pilot seasons and awards seasons, and we always try to meet up when she's here. A few years ago, Francesca invited me to the Golden Globes while she was in town. I accepted the invitation, of course, and I was excited to be a part of something that big and glamorous. The week before the event, we went shopping for dresses.

I got a simple black dress with some jewelry, because that's usually my style, but Francesca, being a beautiful Italian actress, had to make an appearance. We ended up going to several designer showrooms, and stores all over Beverly Hills, and, because she was a well-known Italian actress, we were welcomed and got the best service and a lot of attention. However, the choice was very difficult, and we ended up having to decline several design brands. Every time Francesca would try on a dress, she would make a different remark. The strange thing, though, was that Francesca would tell me, in a serious tone, that she was wondering what her friends would think of her in that dress.

"Anna will say I look awful . . ."

I would ask her why.

"Because Anna sees me as a nobody, and she knows I don't have style . . . she would not wear this color . . ."

And she would take off the dress. Even when she didn't say anything, I could tell what she was thinking about from her expression of disgust. Then, we would move on to the next: next dress, next design, next showroom.

Francesca would look at herself again, saying, "I kind of like this one, but I can imagine what other American actresses would think of me: that I'm pretentious, want to look like a superstar, this dress is too glamorous for me. I'm only an Italian actress who isn't that big yet."

I would tell her that she looked stunning and ask why she should care if those actresses didn't like her.

She would explain, "Yeah, because it's not you who has to see their sarcastic and jealous faces! I can see them in my mind already!"

I remember when she was trying on a beautiful red dress, looking in distress at herself in the mirror.

I was frustrated, too, so I said to her, "Just tell me how you see yourself? What style of dress do you want to see yourself in? What color? What length? Let's find that! But please, stop thinking about what others would say!"

She looked confused, saying: "I don't know. All these people keep showing up in my mind and criticizing me. I even imagine my boyfriend and how he would feel about seeing me in these dresses—he would hate them. They're too sexy, and he's jealous. You know, this is a big event for me, and I have to choose the right dress!"

It didn't take Francesca much longer to find a dress after that. She knew I was tired and frustrated. The dress she got was black, shiny, and very elegant. Francesca wasn't too excited. She thought it was a little too simple, but she decided to go with it, anyway. I was worried that she would later blame me for pressuring her. But, thank God, the second she stepped onto the red carpet and the photographers started taking photos of her, she was over the moon with all the attention. Francesca was thrilled and, at one point, I looked at her and saw her surrounded by three or four men, laughing. The event was super fun. We both had a great time, and almost forgot the struggles of the past week.

This experience with Francesca stuck with me. I never stopped to think about the dialog we have every time we step in front of the mirror. This made me want to start some research on mirrors, how we see ourselves in the mirror, and our overall relationship with them. I soon came to the conclusion that, in our minds, we create an image of other people's opinions of what we look like.

Think about how many times you talk to the reflection in the mirror, hearing other people's thoughts disguised as your own. We judge ourselves based on the idea of how we think others perceive us.

Listening to Francesca's thoughts throughout that week made me start noticing my own. For instance, if I was going to dinner with an old friend, and I was looking at myself in the mirror, I would imagine them criticizing me. I would think that *they* would think my shirt was ugly, or that they would approve of it. The real truth is that *I* don't think I look good in this shirt, therefore, *I* don't think that the other person would like my shirt. I attribute my thoughts to other people.

Again, in our minds, we create an imaginary person and, usually, one with strong opinions about us. In other words, we attribute to others the criticism or praise that are in fact our own. It is not others who judge us, but ourselves.

If I like what I see in the mirror and think of my friend telling me that I look great, I feel happy. If I don't feel comfortable in an outfit and imagine walking up to a group of people that don't like me, I *become* them in my mind and end up feeling insecure. When we see ourselves reflected in the mirror, we create our moods.

The worst part about this phenomenon is that most of it happen unconsciously. The thoughts—whether good or bad—are in your head, so the brain truly believes that the person feels that way about you. Thus, we end up with inexplicable feelings that were fabricated in our minds by these thoughts that we have about ourselves.

What we think and feel when we look in the mirror is a reflection of how we feel about ourselves. Again, the fact that the dissociated image we see in the mirror differs from our perception of self automatically makes us create a version of someone in our heads who will criticize us on our behalf.

When we imagine an important person—let us say a significant other, or a CEO you have a meeting with—you imagine that person in your mind as you look at yourself in the mirror, and will, therefore, know how to dress, behave, and talk to impress them according to the idea of them you have in your mind. You create, in your imagination, a relationship with this person whom you may or may not know that often drastically differs from the reality of the situation.

You are unaware that you do this, so when you actually interact with that person, you are frustrated because they are not behaving according to your plan and act as if they were responsible for the feelings you are left with.

After some research and reflection on this topic, I talked to Francesca about all of it, and she agreed that I had described exactly what her brain was doing as she tried on her dresses for the Golden Globes. She would speculate what other people would think to explain how she felt about herself—an odd phenomenon that happens to all of us, even if we're not aware of it. Francesca didn't remember specifically thinking of other people's opinions on the dresses she was trying on, but she recalled that they just didn't feel right.

6

How Mental Images Shape Our Lives

IF WE THINK about our lives, we will notice that our past is a mere repetition of old experiences, influenced by our current feelings. It is always idealized, like anticipation of the future, influenced by our hopes. We are often not aware of how much time we spend in our heads. We entertain ourselves with thoughts, judgments, speculations, a myriad of images. In fact, there are so many images that fill our minds that it can be confusing to distinguish between them.

Unusually vivid visual memories—also called eidetic images—are retained by our memory and are often attached to emotional experiences. Naturally, all of these images are associated with feelings and sensations. If the feelings are pleasant, then the images will be loved, and there will be a desire to interact with them more often, as they create a sense of pleasure. In any case, it is important to understand where these images come from, to be more aware of what is going on in your mind, and to stop any thoughts that negatively affect your actions.

For example, a client once told me that she remembers herself, at age five or six, running around a beautiful daisy field. She remembers that she felt the urge to simply dive into the middle of the field, surrounded by flowers, and yell, swinging her arms and legs, "I AM HAPPY!" She can easily picture herself back at that moment. She sees herself happy laying on the grass, with her blue dress and her hair tangled around the daisies—and when she remembers, she still feels the same joy she felt that day. Now, how is it possible that she sees this picture?

She can't *actually* see herself, but she clearly does see it. Why? Whenever we encounter things that bring us back to these moments—such as the color of the dress or a bouquet of daisies, in her case—we automatically remember sensations or sights associated with them. Then, we create a representation of that moment, including sounds and our feeling of joy, that we can contain and transform into an image of that event. Of course, this is an example of a happy memory. Later, she told me of another moment in her life.

There is another clear image in her head, but that one is a constant reminder that she was born in a disadvantaged family.

She used to wait outside the door of her house for her parents to come home from the field at night; it usually didn't take them long. However, one night, she waited for them for hours out in the cold. The street was deserted since everyone else was home with their family, and she was alone, miserable, and scared. What if her parents didn't come back? She was very upset. She kept gazing into the end of the street, hoping to see them. She remembers looking at the moths under the streetlight and thinking that it was unfair that they were having fun while she was terrified. Even in this case, the reason she describes that moment so well and in such detail is because the emotions around those circumstances and the bodily sensations are all engraved in her mind. These long-lasting memories are difficult to erase.

We must be aware of these recurring mental images that live in our subconscious, attached to emotions and ready to be attached to our current reality. The mental image is a more or less exact reproduction of the external object that was once absent in the brain. These subconscious images are those that our eyes bring into the brain from our sensory awareness, such as past memories that we are not aware of, or when we are not focused on anything in particular. For example, I may be concentrating and talking on the phone but, in the same moment, looking outside the window and seeing—but not paying attention to—the kids playing in the street before me. My eyes register what they see as I'm talking on the phone, but the images do not reach the threshold of awareness. Thus, these "background" images are stored away in my subconscious.

We think we form ideas consciously. We'd like to think our ideas are our own. They are, but most ideas start in our subconscious. Our mind forms informational archives that include words, images, and emotions that swill together until they're ready for your conscious brain to call upon them. We shouldn't fear our subconscious, for it's our brain's dam—straining a lifetime of information into a digestible trickle.

There are also the thought-images, which are the normal pictures processed every day as part of logical thinking and reasoning. Whether they are clear or confused depends upon the moment of recall. The thought-images are fundamentally descriptive and vary from vague to ultra-vivid.

In contrast, dream pictures, even if remembered correctly, result from the dreamer creating his or her own interpretation of dreams. Even if we don't recall the dreams later, you can be certain that they happened. For some, dream-images are recalled for only a few minutes upon awakening, before they vanish. Dreams are needed in order for the brain to discharge images from our crowded minds.

There is no way for another individual, even research psychologists, to "see" what is in someone else's mind; not even the most vivid descriptions can reflect what is there. Only *you* can make sense of your images, if you learn how to do it. That means only *you* can create the photo album of your life. I like to think of memory as a series of photo albums—scenes from our past that are stored away for us to review. A photo album is an important object that contains our memories and visual experiences. Most pictures in the albums were taken in moments of happiness and are attached to emotional experiences.

An essay titled *The Evolving Self* by Silvano Arieti, the psychiatrist and authority on schizophrenia, describes how he processes mental imagery:

"I close my eyes and visualize my mother. She may not be present, but her image is with me; it stands for her. The image is obviously based on the memory traces of previous perceptions of my mother. My mother then acquires a psychic reality that is not tied to her physical presence."

Arieti goes on to explain how "her image . . . becomes a substitute for the external object" to act as an "inner object." If we believe Arieti's proposal that "image formation is the basis for all higher mental process," we can understand how remembering emotionally charged memories benefit or impinge our mindset.

We see our past as present images with attached emotions, which are often triggered by others—maybe a remark or a criticism that reminds us of something and creates emotional distress that is hard to eliminate from our minds . . . but why? We know that others see us better than we see ourselves, so we automatically assume that whatever they say is more accurate than our own perception of ourselves. Especially during our teenage years, when we don't have an awareness of what we're supposed to look like, criticism is deadly and can provoke strong emotions that last for a long time, if not processed or addressed.

As we grow, our most important memories imprint themselves in our character—our moral, social, and religious attitude toward the world and ourselves. No matter what we do, our brains interpret everything we see, hear, feel, taste and smell, which is stored without discretion, whether good or bad, true or false, joyous or painful. Our brain takes and protects these sensations deep in our subconscious, and we unknowingly carry them throughout our life. Excluding trauma, you can probably make sense of even the most buried episodes of your youth.

In Freudian terms, problems with oneself often arise from subliminal, distorted, and displaced images that are sent to the subconscious mind. These upsetting images are visual memories based on past negative emotions and feelings; they become the mental pictures that give us trouble when we use them as references for our current selves; they're the reason we need a Photo-Image to mitigate the negativity and anchor our feelings to positivity.

When we are children, our mind is not well-formed, and our five senses are not completely controlled by our behavior and reasoning. We internalize everything we see and hear. We absorb and accept the world as other people want us to. It begins with our parents and family members, then teachers and friends . . . we cannot escape this situation. We are also incapable of distinguishing the real world from pictures or imagined events from feelings. No one is immune to these situations, as no one can deny the emotions we still feel as grown-ups. They are the basis for our happiness, character, and success. They are always in our brain, ready to pop up at any moment with any word or sight that we associate with those mental pictures.

For better or worse, you will never forget certain experiences from your childhood, and many of your behaviors from that time forever influence the way you behave. Just like it is hard to forget a time we were bullied or broke-up with a significant other—you probably remember where you were, what was said, and most importantly, how you felt in the moment—our identity from our years of significant change such as our teenage years, our college career, our first years as parents, the first year we felt successful at our jobs follow us. This growth complicates our relationships with friends, acquaintances, and family. With age, we develop heightened feelings of dependence on the opinions of others to influence our own actions and choices. You can always change your location or behavior, but it is near impossible to change the images that go through your mind. If we don't attempt to understand our past and reconcile the concerns we have with it, we will be blind to the source of our pain and remain unable to transform into the person we subconsciously want to be.

One of the most important steps to becoming emotionally complete is by integrating our childhood self into our current self. As previously explained, many of our emotional reactions are involuntary responses to childhood experiences. The behavior we had as a child has a profoundly resounding effect on our behavior as an adult. If not dealt with at the right time, these childhood difficulties can have serious consequences later in life. Looking back, how was your childhood? How well-behaved were you? Do you think about painful episodes of living at home? Anything that makes you angry when you recollect it?

If we understand how our minds work, we will no longer rely on our mental constructions, and we will act with reason. We will not base our well-being on outside things but on our own mental constructs. It is essential to identify and avoid these negative fantasies of yourself. Any imagination or mental picture you create will produce physical conditions and external actions that correspond to your thoughts.

When our mental images connect with our emotions, our facial expressions react and affect our appearance, which in turn affects our mood. If our mental images are pleasant, we are beautiful. Unfortunately, we cannot always rely on the accuracy of our mental images. We must learn how to pay attention to these images, to examine and recognize them, and to be aware of where they can lead us. If they are taking us out of our way, we have to stop them and focus on what matters. This might take a lot of effort because of our natural lack of a strong will.

One of the cognitive psychology's pioneers, Sir Frederic C. Bartlett, wrote about perception in *Remembering: A Study in Experimental and Social Psychology*:

"You must perceive before remembering anything but the real truth is that nothing can be perceived, recognized, or remembered if it hadn't been present before or hadn't been felt another time at the same degree. It's also true that what is recognized, perceived, or remembered in the present becomes a mental image and a thought of an experience in the past."

Essentially, sometimes, we make things up.

A particular episode from a photoshoot has remained stuck in my mind. It was when I went to a secluded house perched atop a hill, featuring tennis courts, a pool, and a large fountain. The great room had all kinds of collections statues, vases, and masks from around the world. The home was over-the-top, even for Beverly Hills.

The actress was beautiful, charming, welcoming, and enthusiastic to share her home and take pictures for the magazine spread. I was essentially at liberty to take pictures wherever I pleased.

While she was upstairs preparing for the shoot, my assistant prepared the lighting, and I chose a large corner with a stunning view of the garden, the pool, and the city below. It was clearly the ideal spot. We would seat her on a soft blue couch by a huge coffee table that was filled with a collection of twenty-some figurines, each one representing a moment of daily activity in a farm village. There was a cute boy shining shoes, a flower girl, men working in the field, women washing clothes, a smiling mailman, children running and playing piano, chickens, ducks, a cow, and a horse. The whole collection was beautiful and probably extremely expensive.

I noted that the glass table was quite dusty and covered in cigarette ashes and rings left from drinks. This was strange as the rest of the house was completely spotless. I advised my assistant to be careful and clean up the coffee table and prepare the lights while I went upstairs to check on my client. We chatted and laughed and proceeded downstairs where everything was ready to begin the photoshoot.

She moved toward the coffee table. Suddenly, she stopped cold and put her hand to her mouth. She asked incredulously what we had done to her coffee table knick-knacks. We thought maybe we had broken something, but since we hadn't, we were dumbfounded at her reaction.

She asked if my assistant or I had moved the collection and reprimanded us, saying, "How dare you!"

I explained that it was necessary in order to remove the dust and ashes for the shoot. She calmed down, and we started the session, but she had already shown negative feelings, and her smile was difficult to recapture. She was not collaborative, and she had no energy. All the pleasure and anticipation were gone. This made me freeze up too. My assistant and I were terrified.

After an hour, she said she had a headache and—trying to be polite—she said we could maybe reschedule for another day. I knew at that point that there would never be another day and that the shoot was over, but, unfortunately, not finished. However, it was futile to continue, as the fruits of our labor would be useless. The pictures I had taken were useless, too. We apologized a lot and then we left.

I was confused and upset to have not completed the job. The next morning, she called, and I didn't want to answer as I was still upset. Yet, she called again and again. When I finally answered, she apologized profusely and insisted on explaining her overreaction. She proposed to meet me for an early lunch, and I agreed.

She explained that the ceramic figurines represented her village when she was young, and each piece was put in place the way that she remembered it—the old woman looking toward the church, the milk-men toward the house of her friend, the chicks next to the lady who was feeding them, and so on. What bothered her most was the angry duck with the long neck that was biting the woman's behind. The woman was her mother! The duck was supposed to bite the boy next to the fountain! I was stunned. Was she kidding me? I obviously hadn't attached that much meaning to the figurines and hadn't realized what I had done.

I scratched my head, speechless. I asked her which figurine represented her in that scene, and she said, "I was the girl dancing next to the river with the flowers!"

She immediately regressed to become that little girl and continued talking in a childish voice.

She said that it was all in her mind and that she tried to recreate those happy childhood scenes of long ago with the figurines in the village. The actual village doesn't exist, anymore. Now, the river has dried up, and there's a big freeway intersection instead.

She said, "Only a few people know about what that collection means to me, and I get upset when someone moves it. Even my housekeeper can't clean up the coffee table. I forgot to say anything to you, but you happened to pick that very spot for the shoot. I need to apologize, and I realize that my reaction was too strong."

What could I say? I felt sorry for her. I was sympathetic and recognized that she had a deep-rooted problem that she needed to address. I reassured her that I would not use any of the pictures taken. She was grateful and then said goodbye. I didn't hear from her for a couple of years; I didn't even see her in the movies or a magazine. I lost sight of her but couldn't forget the episode.

One day, she called to say that she had heard about Photo-Image from friends and wanted to schedule a session. I was hesitant at first, saying that I was too busy and that I really didn't think it would be a good idea, based on our past experience. She insisted. This time, she came to my home studio, and we did a great shoot. She understood exactly the purpose of my theory. It was like working with a completely different person.

This is the email that I received along with a Christmas wish:

"This morning I was going to put up my Christmas tree, and I went to my closet to find all the ornaments. I also found the big box that contains the ceramic figurines that you know very well and that I stored after my psychotherapist advised me to. Today, I opened the box and saw the angry duck—you remember the one that was biting my mother? I started to laugh and laugh. Thinking about you, I continued searching for the dancing girl and I took it and went to the living room and saw my Photo-Image. I have never been so aware of who I am in my life. Looking at my image and having the little figurine in my hand was the realization that I'm the happy little girl inside. I see that I have grown up to be genuine, spontaneous, capable, generous, and beautiful. I have never felt so good about myself and I feel fully aware and present. With a deep breath, I put everything back in the box, all the figurines, and I'm sure that I really don't need them anymore. I know who I am and now know what I want. I think that

I will sell the collection. Finally, I am myself. Merry Christmas and I wish that you can reach many people with your kind and gentle Photo-Image. Thank you."

How to Put the Past Away

Every mental image we have is connected to emotions that belong not to us, but to our past. We tend to see the past in the present, we but cannot let it influence our future. Any time we encounter negative feelings associated with memories, we become distressed and distracted from the present moment. Something needs to be done about that.

The only way to change how we respond to negative emotions is to confront what made us first feel them. You can't ever forget your past; what you can do is learn to accept it. We often use events from the past to label ourselves, using them as an excuse to develop self-rejection. However, feeling guilty for past events can have serious effects on your present. That is why it is crucial to develop compassion for yourself. We often hear that we should be compassionate to others, but directing compassion onto yourself is just as important, if not more.

By developing compassion, you will finally be able to forgive. True forgiveness means letting go of the past, cultivating self-respect, and looking to a better future. Self-awareness facilitates self-acceptance; you can recall the past to profit from it. Do not take too long focusing on the future either, or it will take you away from the present. Succeeding in awareness is essential to develop the ability to understand the relationship between your past and your present. Once you have accepted and experienced who you are, you will abandon all ideas of who you should be. Then, you will be aware and ready to accomplish more and to grow to your full potential.

I have advised some of my clients to sort their memories by creating a folder and organizing their mental images, much like we used to do with physical albums in the past. This organization is important because we validate our lives by making sense of what we had, what we want, where we take our ideas from, and where we want to go next. Photo-imagery allows us to take charge of the images in our life and take control of the photo album of our life.

This is a helpful tip when you are dealing with resentment and negativity: Create a folder on your computer and write down all bad memories you can remember in a document—your shame, resentment, guilt, and every bit of negative imagery you can find. You can write it down in metaphors, stories, or symbols that represent your bad memory. You can also describe the memory and its environment in great detail. You can do it all at once or go back to the folder as soon as the negative feelings arise. As long as you know that the past has a place to stay that's not in your body or mind but outside of yourself, you will be able to let go of negativity.

Then, close that folder and put it somewhere you won't see it: either off the desktop or transferred to an external drive. If some memory or thought comes out from that folder, make sure to put it back, recognizing that these thoughts belong to a place called "The Past." If you are ever nostalgic and need to feel the pain again—which will happen, as we can become attached to our pain—open the folder and check the files. Feel the pain again and acknowledge it. Your memories will always remain yours. Recognize that your past contributes to who you are—the better you—and be thankful. Then, put it back in its place again and forget about it. Keep everything far away from today's reality and away from your mind's eye.

Another way of controlling how negative emotions affect you is by visualizing the person or action in your mind that has caused you pain. Analyze the details of your memory in order to create the most realistic image possible: what were the colors, the sounds, the smells, the furniture, the taste. Then, feel all the negative emotions that follow—the anger, shame, resentment, fear—and attribute it to that image, detached from you. Transfer these feelings into the image in your head with every breath. Allow yourself to watch that memory in the third person. Once the emotions attached to that memory are brought back and feel very real, imagine a dimmer light switch in your mind. Begin turning the switch and imagine the memory slowly fading and, with it, all the emotions attached to it. Slowly, the light will go out. Do this as many times as needed, and, eventually, you will no longer feel anything when you think of that memory. This exercise will take time. It isn't possible to be able to turn the light off on this memory so easily or quickly. That is why we use a dimmer.

7

The Self as a Visual Self

As a native Italian speaker, one of the hardest English words for me to understand was "self."

In Italian, the word "self" is untranslatable.

The word *"io,"* means "I"; *"me stesso"* is "myself"; *"la mia identita,"* "my identity"; *"la mia imagine,"* "my image"; *"la mia persona,"* "my person."

There are many other possessive statements used to describe what, in English, is known as "self."

Then I realized that, in English, the self wasn't much more tangible. It is impossible to identify it or give it a single definition. We can say that it is both a reflection of the idea we have about our being as well as a construction of ideas about our behaviors and characteristics, including feelings and consciousness itself.

The self is a complex concept and is a common subject of philosophy, psychology, sociology, neuroscience, religion, and spirituality, all being an attempt to understand the human mind and the complexity of the self.

Consider how many times throughout human history the concept of self has evolved and changed meaning.

Let us start with one of the most famous sayings in history, "Know thyself," inscribed in the front door of the ancient Greek Temple of Apollo at Delphi dating from the fourth century BC. When asked what the most difficult thing in life was, the early Greek philosopher Thales responded, "To know thyself."

A couple of centuries earlier, in India, the topic of the self appeared in the *Upanishads,* which are embedded in the *Vedas,* the oldest of Hinduism's religious scriptures. It was also part of the Confucian thoughts in China. The self is a result of the human consciousness's interest in self-reflection and our will to identify and to understand ourselves.

In 483 BCE, the self was prominent in the philosophy of Siddhartha Gautama Buddha:

"There is no self, it is the thought that thinks, there is no thinker behind the thought. In the same way, it is wisdom, realization, that realizes. There is no other self behind the realization."

Buddha's concept of the self, identity, self-observation, and introspection is still of interest to behavior and social science researchers.

Another unique view of the self comes after a few millennia, when theological literature interpreted the self as evil and selfish. The self was seen as immoral and as an interference between body and spiritual life.

Soon after the renaissance, René Descartes reintroduced the concept of the "individual self" in his book, *Discourse on the Method* (1637), which was one of my main inspirations for writing this book. His concept of self is still being discussed today, as well as the idea of Cartesian Dualism.

In his extensive description of the self, philosopher John Locke describes persona and identity—not accounting for the soul or spirit—and defines these qualities of the self as how a person takes himself into "consideration." In *An Essay Concerning Human Understanding*, he offers this as a definition of the self:

"Conscious thinking thing, which is sensible, or conscious of pleasure and pain, capable of happiness or misery, and so is concerned for itself, as far as that consciousness extends."

Locke's philosophy is believed to be the origin of our current ideas on self and identity. He went against both Christian and Cartesian philosophy when he stated that the mind was a "tabula rasa," a blank slate, meaning that we are born without innate ideas.

Philosopher and psychologist William James proposed a more direct definition of the self in his work, *The Principles of Psychology,* where he defines the self as composed of the following four constituents: The material self, the social self, the spiritual self, and the pure ego. For James, the material self, the social self, and the spiritual self were all part of the "me" self that refers to the qualities or beliefs a person has that are formed from life experiences. On the other hand, he categorized the pure ego as the "I" self that is essentially the human mind as we know it.

Similarly, psychoanalyst Sigmund Freud's concept of the id, ego, and superego in the last century separates the components of the self. This had a great influence on the generations of thinkers who came after him. Psychoanalysis continues to influence the psychological and sociological studies that are practiced today.

In his book, *Treating the Self: Elements of Clinical Self-Psychology,* Ernest S. Wolf describes the self as containing a past, present, and future. Despite the passage of time, we feel that we remain the same, though a simple analysis of ourselves over the years will reveal how we've changed.

From the strictly scientific perspective of his critically acclaimed book, *Synaptic Self: How Our Brains Become Who We Are*, neurologist Joseph Le Doux describes the self as "the essence of who you are, [that] reflects patterns of interconnectivity between neurons in your brain. Connections between neurons, known as synapses, are the main channels of information flow and storage in the brain. Most of what the brain does is accomplished by synaptic transmission between neurons, and by calling upon the information encoded by past transmission across synapses."

He argues that everything that composes our sense of personality, or "self," is neural in nature—as opposed to psychological, metaphysical, or moral—and that the psychological, social, moral, aesthetic, or spiritual self is realized as a synaptic process of information storage. Fundamentally, he believes the self is comprised of the neuron connections that define cognitive ability.

Neurologist Antonio Damasio relates the concept of the "autobiographical self" to the development of personal, autobiographical memory in his book, *The Feeling of What Happens: Body and Emotion in the Making of Consciousness*. The "autobiographical self is based on autobiographical memory, which is constituted by implicit memories of multiple instances of individual experience of the past and of the anticipated future." For Damasio, the self is a set of memories that infuses us with awareness of ourselves and who we are. He applies significant importance to the body as the means through which we create memory and how we apply it to the idea of the self.

In line with this idea, sociologist Anthony Giddens describes the self, in his book, *Modernity and Self-Identity,* as an "identity [that] is not a distinctive trait, or even a collection of traits, possessed by the individual. It is the self as reflexively understood by the person in terms of his or her biography." Giddens proposes that the self is "embodied" and makes the claim that the "body is at the very origin of the original explorations of the world." For Giddens, the self is very much a part of the body. Giddens has acknowledged, somewhat more extensively than others, the role of the "body-self" in the formulation of identity.

Erving Goffman, a sociologist, also discusses the importance of the body-self in his book, *The Presentation of Self in Everyday Life,* in which he makes the point that we actively and routinely put on a performance of who we are "for the benefit of other people."

Furthermore, what this is saying is that the self is our body, but at the same time, we are also our bodies. To understand this, we how the foundation of a human is a material unit.

The foundation of a human is a material unit—an object in time and space. We can never fully see this self because we are limited to what lies before our field of vision: for example, our hands. The use of our hands and fingers separates us from the rest of the animal world, along with the size of our highly developed brain. The hands are in front of our eyes so that we can see what we are doing and creating in our active life. We see our feet from above to observe how we are able to walk, dance, or move. Step-by-step, we are able to see how to avoid obstacles. Step-by-step, with some type of internal feedback—be it visual, auditory, or other—we can train our bodies to perform incredible feats.

The Importance of Self-Image Perception

In the 1970s, 80s, and 90s, overlapping fragments within the psychological realm related to the self came back, due to the humanistic approach that academic psychology and behavioral science had at the time. Their popularity was enormous. Thousands of books, lectures, and seminars spread across the country, giving birth to the self-help book mania that is still going strong today. The terms self-awareness, self-esteem, self-control, self-affirmation, etc. were popularized around this time.

I SEE MYSELF, THEREFORE I AM

The self-esteem movement, in particular, took off across America with the incentive of the state of California in 1986 that established a task force to improve self-esteem in the workplace and in schools. Workshops dominated workplaces, and school curriculums were expanded to teach children the importance of cultivating positive self-esteem. To many, it seemed to be a sound answer to many of the social problems that troubled society.

In the national spotlight, self-image is often ignored, despite being as important as—if not more important than—self-esteem. It is fundamentally rooted in everything we experience. A positive self-image is crucial as part of a positive self-esteem, determining our degree of happiness, fulfillment, success, mental health, emotional stability, and overall satisfaction of life. The only limits to your life achievements have been defined by the limits your self-image puts on you. If we care about ourselves, it's our responsibility to examine our self-image in order to make every attempt to improve it. Besides, low self-esteem and poor self-image have long been associated with a whole range of psychological problems, and it is necessary to counter the passive individual that depends heavily on the social world to build self-image. We should develop a self-image that is more based on our own evaluations rather than how we believe others look at us.

To a certain extent, your self-image is the mental picture you have of yourself. It is made up of a combination of all of the memories, feelings, actions, relationships, images, tastes, and sounds you have experienced throughout your life that you use to identify yourself. These feelings and emotions, whether negative or positive, contribute to your self-image. These experiences include your perception of your strengths and weaknesses, your physical beauty and shortcomings, and your intellectual ability. Most importantly, your self-image is also based on how you see yourself in relation to others.

Everyone wants to be liked and appreciated for their talents and personality. However, if we have a weak self-image, and if we believe that the opinions of others are more important than our own, we end up living our lives in accordance with other people's expectations. Sometimes, others' evaluations mean more to us than our own. This is quite a distressing thought since it implies that others' opinions of you can run your life.

When your ideal self and your self-image are consistent, you will have a realistic sense of self-worth and a glowing self-esteem. Conversely, when your ideal self and your self-image are inconsistent, you will experience a continuous stream of negativity in your mind. This is the overwhelmingly more common case. Don't worry if you feel this negativity, as there is a solution: If you have a clear self-image, you can use it as a motivational tool to anchor yourself and fuel your beliefs with certainty.

Know that you cannot possibly have positive self-esteem without having a positive self-image. Even if you wear a fake smile and appear as if you are totally fine, your truth is not going to change. Just like how your past will always affect your present until you address it, you cannot address your self-esteem without first considering your self-image.

It should come as no surprise to you that your self-image is threatened by the beauty standards of the media. When you compare yourself to the beautiful cover models who have had every imperfection digitally removed, you create unrealistic standards for yourself and that will damage both your self-image and self-esteem.

Who am I? How do I look? How important am I? How am I doing? Where do I go?

By answering these questions, you create a structure to determine your success or failure, the amount of joy or sadness you should experience, and the level of satisfaction you have with your general quality of life. If you are not willing to understand what is going on in your mind, you could not possibly be able to understand yourself or achieve your true desires, though you may achieve plenty of desires you believe to be true. Self-observation and reflection play critical roles in unraveling the mysteries of your self-image and discovering what it is that you truly believe you must do in order to make your life outstanding and worthwhile.

Developing a sturdy self-image will benefit you by instilling within you a feeling of optimism for the future without insecurity and instead with the power to effortlessly cope with everyday problems. A strong self-image will ground you in a way nobody can undo. Once you see yourself properly, you will have more confidence, self-image, self-esteem, and self-knowledge than ever before. The space in your mind that was once bound by insecurity will become the center of your vision. You will see a clear path to your goals and a renewed sense of accomplishment on your life's quest to fulfillment.

I SEE MYSELF, THEREFORE I AM

As you deconstruct your self-image, you may feel compelled to talk about the mental pictures you will realize you have had of yourself and the reasons you feel the way you do about your appearance. You will remember traumatic experiences that you would rather repress, and you will find it tolling to work through the pain. However, only by pressing into these issues will you understand how you have become who you are. Once you have unblocked these parts of your brain, you will understand how your brain went on to create the image you had in the first place. From there, you will be able to change your perspective to that of a much happier reality.

Early one morning, I received a phone call from a French magazine. The magazine publisher said they have an actress in LA, Natalia, who is in need of some starter headshots. He gave her my number and said she would get in touch with me and would pay my fee herself. A week or so later, on a Saturday, my assistant and I arrived at her address in Beverly Hills. The house was huge, and a maid in uniform opened the door. As we came in, I looked up and saw Natalia. She gracefully walked down the long-curved stairway wearing jeans and a T-shirt. She looked so young! Long black hair, dark vivid eyes, and a pretty smile. We chatted for a while about movies and the industry, and you could truly hear the excitement in her voice as she talked about her passions to acting and become an actress.

After Natalia's hair and makeup were done, we walked over to her closet to figure out what she was going to wear for the shoot. We entered a massive room, and I could not believe my eyes. The clothes hung lined up to the ceiling on all sides of the closet. Natalia pushed a button on the wall, and the clothes began to move up, down, and go back and forth. It was unbelievable! I started to laugh to myself about how a twenty-three-year-old girl could have so many clothes next to a smaller room with all kinds of shoes and bags I had never seen even in the house of celebrities. A few minutes later, she talked into the intercom, and an armed guard showed up. He moved a panel and opened a safe. She grabbed a few sets of earrings and a necklace from there and told me to choose what I liked from the pile of expensive jewelry. While she was getting ready, I walked downstairs to get ready for the shoot, and my assistant was reading a magazine. He looked up and handed it to me. The girl from upstairs was on the cover of an illustrated French magazine, the same one that had brought us together, to begin with. Natalia was the daughter of a famous European billionaire. She eventually came back down. I didn't say anything to her or ask any questions about who she was, and we began to shoot.

Later in the evening, as we were wrapping up and my assistant had already left, Natalia asked me if I wanted to stay and order a pizza. We were both tired and hungry, and there were no bodyguards or maids insight. I accepted. She asked me what kind of pizza to order, and I told her she could order whatever she likes. I could eat anything; I was starving and tired. As we waited for the food to arrive, I sat down on the floor collecting my films and cleaning up. The pizza arrived after some time, and that brought another surprise: she had ordered ten different pizzas from a famous, expensive Italian restaurant. She sat down right next to me on the floor and told the delivery girl to place the pizza boxes around us on the floor. Burrata, truffles, caviar, salmon—you name it.

"Whatever I like," she said, laughing. "Now, you can choose."

It was like a scene from a movie.

I am a blunt person, so as we were eating and talking, I felt compelled to ask her *why* she was sitting on the floor eating pizza with me on a Saturday night when she could be out having a good time with handsome guys or her girlfriends.

"When I was around your age, in Rome, it wasn't unusual for my friends and me to party all night in discotheques until early morning and then wait for our favorite bakery to open as soon as the first batch of croissants were ready. They were always so warm, and the fresh scent of bread filled the air, mixing with the breezy air of dawn as the sun rose above the rooftops of Rome—"

Before I could even finish my last sentence, Natalia had inched closer to me, put her head on my chest, and started sobbing. I was frozen.

I asked her if everything was OK and tried to console her, somehow.

"I don't have anybody to go out with," she told me. "I only have a few friends here, and most of them aren't available at night. I miss my family. They got divorced when I was younger . . ."

It felt strange to hear her say these things; it was almost hard to believe that someone who has everything was still so lonely and sad.

"Trust me, it's hard for me to be a normal person. I can't just walk around with armed bodyguards all the time. It intimidates people. My friends never seem to want to hang out. They only do it at parties to show me off as some trophy."

I looked at her, and she stared back at me.

"I'm sorry, I don't know why I'm telling you any of this. We barely know each other; your story makes me think of how wonderful it would be to have fun and be free. Sorry for my emotional burst. Maybe I just needed someone who doesn't know who I am to confide in . . . well, *I* don't even know who I am! I know I'm rich, but what else? I just want to be liked and treated like any other person would want to be treated."

Natalia wiped her eyes and continued.

"When I see myself in the mirror, all that I can see is the image of an inadequate little girl who will never be good enough. I see my own reflection in the same way I imagine other people see me, with dislike and dissatisfaction. You know," she said with a soft voice, "when I go to Rodeo Drive with my bodyguards and spend thousands of dollars at the stores, everyone pretends to love me. They ask to take photos with me and act as if I were the most beautiful person in the world . . . but I know that they're fake. They know who I am. But honestly, who am I?"

She looks at me. At this point, she got up to grab a bottle of wine. We drank some of it, and that made her more comfortable.

"Sometimes, I have the need to sneak away from my bodyguards. I go to the mall wearing no makeup, wearing a T-shirt and jeans, just to feel like a normal person. I smile to others, and try to appear friendly, but people stare back with such indifference and coldness. I feel as though I am looking at myself in the mirror and that I'm right to think that I am inadequate and unworthy. I feel my anger growing as I start to despise everyone around me. I start thinking, 'You're only treating me like this because you don't know who I am!' But I know how silly I am for feeling the need to be treated like a good person and be respected. For what reason? Just because I'm one of the richest girls in Europe?

"Truthfully, what I want more than anything is to be surrounded by people that want to have me around and who appreciate me for who I am. I'm lucky to have a shoulder to cry on, tonight, someone who can listen to me without lecturing me or diagnosing what is wrong with me. I'm terribly sorry to bring the mood down, but I just can't help feel this immense sadness right now."

I tried to console her, but she turned away and said, "I'm aware that you didn't know who I was until you saw the cover of the magazine. I believe that your attitude toward me would have changed after that, but I was glad it didn't. You truly treated me with genuine kindness and respect, even encouraging me to be myself in the photographs. Tonight, we sat on the floor together, enjoying way too much pizza, and we laughed. I felt good and accepted for who I am for the first time in a long time. Thank you for that."

I had a lot to think about after that night with Natalia. I knew I had to write down some observations of what she told me. I had never heard someone explain their feelings in such a spontaneous way like she did, nor had I thought about her struggles myself. I called her the next day, because I had left some equipment behind the night before since I was tired and it was very late when I left.

Then, I said to her, "I was touched by your story. Now, I realize we don't know each other very well, but what you expressed last night about yourself is extremely important for my studies about the Photo-Image. I would love to talk more about how you see yourself, your relationship with the mirror, and the Photo-Image."

She was so happy and excited that she wanted to do it right then and there. Even though I was tired, the shoot was very revealing. By the end of it, her eyes were sparkling, and her smile was contagious. She told me she hadn't felt that good and confident in a long time. The power of self-image lies in having a clear and accurate interpretation of it in our mind, otherwise, the confusion brought on by how others see you can prove to distance you from who you really are. As seen through Natalia's account, seeing yourself is knowing yourself.

The Self as a Visual Identity

Looking down, women can see their bust—a constant reminder of femininity and female identity. This visual is a reminder of a woman's ability to nurse her child and her incredible ability to procreate, which can give her a strong sense of permanence. When men look down at their bodies, they see their genitals and recognize their function and identity as men with qualities of virility, power, endurance, strength, and durability. Because we never see them, we seldom think about the importance of the sensory receptors on our head. The sockets house our eyes, the holes of our ears that allow us to hear, the two openings of the nose that allow us to breathe, the aperture of the mouth that allows us not only to breathe, taste, and nourish ourselves, but communicate as well. We sometimes acknowledge our other openings—the ones that serve a sexual purpose and the others that discharge waste. This is important because we have to be aware of what we put into our bodies and brains.

These critical life-permitting features are not directly visible to you, but if you pay attention to all of your openings at once, you may awaken a great sense of your body that reminds you that you are a living organism. Try to feel all your whole body at once, and you will feel an awareness of your vital parts and awaken to the knowledge that you are a breathing life force of nature.

Beyond your body, your self is composed of what you bring with it—your genetics, name, and ethnicity. Consider how we prove our identities with photos, as we do when we display in a passport or driver's license, and how they play a defining role in our psychological identification that distinguishes ourselves from other people. Even though photos are the most efficient ways to define ourselves, we know we are also our personal belief systems, our unique intelligence, and our reasoning.

Psychologically speaking, there are distinct terms used to describe the parts of self.

First, our self-concept is our general, abstract idea of who we are based on qualities such as sexuality, racial identity, or gender role. It is your whole set of attitudes and beliefs combined with the self-image, ideal self, self-esteem, self-identity, and self-awareness of who you are as a person. Self-concept is more of a scientific term than an emotional one. Self-image, on the other hand, is how you *see* yourself: your physical appearance and your self-perception.

The way we relate to others is our self-identity. For example, the sense of nationality and cultural affiliation are factors of self-identity. This definition of the self also includes the answer to the bigger question of "Who are you?" such as name, age, weight, and other qualities that give a person validation in relation to other people. The sense of self-identity also depends on the different stages we enter in life, like childhood and adult milestones.

Self-esteem, one of the most important parts of the self, is an evaluation of how much you accept or approve of yourself or an attachment to yourself as a person. Of course, this can be positive or negative and is always susceptible to change depending on our own actions and the actions of those around us. Self-esteem is important for our survival. Feeling like you are worthy of living is a primary motivating factor in your life. You should never feel stuck with the person you are. Understand that self-esteem is based on our attitude toward ourselves. Good family relationships and good moral standards, as well as the way you see yourself, all directly affect how you feel at any given day.

How you wish to be, or think you should be, is your ideal self. This is shaped by your life experiences, cultural values, the opinions of others, and traits you admire in role models.

Today's self is never the same as last year's self, nor will it be the same self several years in the future. Our ability to change facilitates our ability to divide ourselves over periods of time, which allows room for self-doubt to come into play. Coupled with the fact that we constantly seek confirmation from others in the form of praise, acceptance, or even mere acknowledgment, we are driven to hang onto any defining factors we can. It is no surprise then how a simple look—or a lack of one—can transform how we feel.

We can reach an understanding of who we are through the recognition of our visual presence. To exist and feel alive, it is important to see your image and everything it represents. Through understanding our appearance, we can understand how we are reflecting our internal world of emotion through our expressions, behavior, and body language as well as recognize the emotions of those around us. We must be aware of how outside judgments distort our interpretation of who we are as we try to recognize ourselves. To become aware of your visual presence is to become aware of your true self—existing outside of our constructs, our self-imposed ideals, and our false characteristics—and to see the truth of your reality as a unique human being.

Only you are yourself. This simple understanding is necessary to achieve a higher level of confidence in yourself and your beauty. If you care about what others think about you and try to please them, you may betray yourself. If their facial expressions hint that they are reacting poorly to the way you look, you might feel there is something wrong with you, dislike yourself, and, in turn, feel miserable.

I SEE MYSELF, THEREFORE I AM

Remember a time when someone's facial expression manipulated your emotions, or when a coworker gave you a bad look and you suddenly felt different. Perhaps you couldn't focus for the rest of the day, or maybe you couldn't even sleep well that night all, because you became aware that someone dislikes you, just because of a facial expression. Maybe there was a time when someone important ignored you and your need to be seen by them wasn't met. You felt a lack of acknowledgment, and your honor was somehow robbed as your presence went unnoticed. These experiences add to the way you see yourself. Since we are always internalizing our experiences and adding them to our identities, our self-concept is constantly being transformed.

If we agree with Joseph Le Doux's theory of the synaptic self—which says we're the physical, psychological, social, moral, and autobiographical information contained in the interconnectivity between our neurons—we will find that the Photo-Image adds to his theory of visual identity. As he said, "Our brains become who we are."

8

Understanding Others to Understand Yourself

Consider the impact other people's reactions to you or your actions have on how you perceive the value or importance of your actions, thoughts, expressions, etc. We often rely on unspoken and subtle social cues or reactions from others to understand our own behavior and standing in a given situation. This feeds into your self-image and how you grow to define yourself. A nasty look from someone you esteem might make you feel negative about yourself. Miscommunication and misinterpretation could have detrimental effects that you internalize and project onto your self-image. That is why, learning the different ways individuals learn, inform themselves, and communicate is helpful in identifying when someone's unrelated scowl after you share your opinion about something important to you isn't related to who you are and is something you shouldn't allow to impact how you see yourself.

In general, we perceive through these five sensory channels: Visual, auditory, kinesthetic (feeling), olfactory (relating to smell), and gustatory (taste), with the first three being the most prominently depended on. Understanding which sense a person prefers is as easy as paying attention to the words they use in describing experiences.

A person who prefers visual representation will use visual words like see, look, watch, bright, colorful, clear, "I see what you're saying," or "I can picture that." People who prefer visuals are often beauty-centric as painters, architects, strategists, graphic designers, fashion designers, craftspeople, novelists, cinematographers. and photographers.

A person who prefers auditory representations will use words like hear, listen, sound, resonate, click, say, rings a bell, "I hear you," or "Sounds good." Philosophers, scholars, psychologists, intellectuals, musicians, and composers are often auditory people who rely on expression of concepts through sound or the meaning of specific words.

A person who prefers kinesthetic representation will use words like feel, handle, touch, rough, heavy, hold, fills me with, "I feel that," or "Feels good." Kinesthetic types include doctors, athletes, dancers, physiotherapists, nutritionists, manufacturers, and people who use touch and feeling to experience the world. They may think less in terms of words and more in terms of action and duty.

We all possess these modes of thinking and learning, and there is only a chance you favor one, but you will notice a natural ease interacting with someone who prefers the same mode.

To further elaborate, geniuses are found to often exhibit an equal percentage of all three dominant modes of thinking. Leonardo Da Vinci displayed visuals through painting, kinesthetic because he practiced early forms of surgery—dissecting corpses with his hands—and auditory because he was both a writer and musician (who played the flute and the lyre).

We can also see how Visual, Auditory, and Kinesthetic modes of thinking work in harmony in taking a look at how Amadeus Mozart describes his creative process:

"When I am, as it were, completely myself, entirely alone, and of good cheer; say traveling in a carriage, or walking after a good meal, or during the night when I cannot sleep; it is on such occasions that my ideas flow best and most abundantly. Whence and how they come, I know not; nor can I force them. Those pleasures that please me I retain in my memory and am accustomed, as I have been told, to hum them to myself. If I continue in this way, it soon occurs to me, how I may turn this or that morsel to account, so as to make a good dish of it, that is to say, agreeably to the rules of counterpoint, to the peculiarities of the various instruments, etc. All this fires my soul, and provided

I SEE MYSELF, THEREFORE I AM

I am not disturbed, my subject enlarges itself, becomes methodized and defined, and the whole, though it is long, stands almost finished and complete in my mind, so that I can survey it, like a picture or a beautiful statue, at a glance. Nor do I hear in my imagination the part successively, but I hear them, as it were, all at once . . . When I proceed to write down my ideas, I take out of the bag of my memory, if I may use that phrase, what has been previously collected into it, in the way I have mentioned. For this reason, the committing to paper is done quickly enough, for everything is, as I said before, already finished; and it rarely differs on paper from what it was in my imagination."

(On Mozart, edited by James M. Morris)

This simplified categorizing of how we learn and communicate can be a helpful tool in connecting with others and learning to not take their reactions to our opinions and actions personally. Building rapport with others is also possible when we can understand their preferred mode of thinking and how their communication style is defined by effect. When you understand the reasoning behind others' actions and opinions of you, you can separate their influence from how you interpret who you are.

Here is a simple test that you can use to discern your thinking modality. Understanding your thinking modality allows you to expand your perspective—first notice how you think, then think about something a different way. It is possible you may notice something that becomes important to you as you pay more attention or use your knowledge to converse more meaningfully with people with other modalities.

QUALITIES - V.A.K

VISUAL	AUDITORY	KINESTHETIC
"see"	"hear"	"grasp"
"look"	"listen"	"touch"
"sight"	"sound"	"feeling"
"clear"	"resonant"	"solid"
"bright"	"loud"	"heavy"
"picture"	"word"	"handle"
"hazy"	"noisy"	"rough"
"brings to light"	"rings a bell"	"connects"
"show"	"tell"	"move"

VAK Learning Styles Test

- **When I think about a friend, I:**
  a. see their face in my mind
  b. recall a conversation we had
  c. remember how they make me feel

- **I usually buy new clothes based on:**
  a. how they look
  b. how much they cost
  c. how the fabric feels

- **I feel most inspired by:**
  a. beautiful sights, art, performances
  b. Music, concerts, speeches
  c. physical endurance, sports, crafts

- **When telling a story, I:**
  a. describe the events in visual detail
  b. explain the events in sequence
  c. use gestures and describe emotions

- **My friends would say that I:**
  a. have good taste
  b. am a good listener
  c. make them feel good

- **What touches me most about a film is:**
  a. the cinematography
  b. the dialogue, or musical score
  c. the feelings it inspires

- **I enjoy learning about other countries by:**
  a. their art and museums
  b. their language and history
  c. their food and customs

- **To learn a new recipe I first:**
  a. look up pictures
  b. read the directions
  c. experiment how to make it myself

- **I am most confident about:**
  a. my sense of style and presence
  b. my intellect and knowledge
  c. my skill and ability

Add your score

a	b	c
☐	☐	☐
☐	☐	☐
☐	☐	☐
☐	☐	☐
☐	☐	☐
☐	☐	☐
☐	☐	☐
☐	☐	☐
☐	☐	☐
Visual	Auditory	Kinesthetic

9

Emotions as Images

"**Y**OU DON'T NEED knowledge to understand the emotions." -Nico Frijda, *The Emotions: Studies in Emotion and Social Interaction*

Emotions flavor our lives; they can make the tragedy a turning point or a victory a loss. Our greatest strengths and weaknesses stem from the emotions we put into them. Our emotions let us fly from the ground or trap us in dark cells of our mind. The power emotions have over us stems from our confusion as to what they are, how they work, and where they come from. Once we understand our emotional source, we can treat them kindly and keep them from spinning out of control. Too often, we allow our emotions power over ourselves. Let's consider the words of some brilliant psychologists who shed light on the significant role emotions play in our lives.

We look to renowned psychologists for insight:

"*Once conflicted emotions are clearly labeled and expressed, the useful tool of rational thought is available for resolving as much of the conflict as possible and for accepting realistic limitations. Unfortunately, we do not have a clear map for a given personality to follow in working through conflict, trauma, and losses. But we do recognize the importance of facial expressions. The emotions are the most powerful factor in our life. Most importantly, we can't isolate the emotions from the rest of the mental process including mental imagery, memory, unconscious, sensation, and perception.*" - Robert White, *The Abnormal Personality*

"*It's impossible for feelings to happen on their own. Emotions and sensations can only be understood when seen how they work in our own bodies. Feelings can be stimulated from the outside, but only the individual can really know what he or she is feeling."* - Herbert Spencer, *The Principles of Psychology*

Their insight into emotion was significant, but I believe William James' book *The Principles of Psychology* better captures the idea that emotions cannot exist outside of the body. James contests the idea of a separation between emotions and the body, claiming "a purely disembodied human emotion is a nonentity."

What James means is that if we attempt to remove any emotion from its origin—i.e., crying when feeling sad—we are left with mere "unfeeling cognition." He proposed that emotions only exist when we express their physical stimulation; that is, when we express them through our face and body. According to James, emotions are "sensational processes due to inward currents set up by physical happenings," and so, whatever passions or moods we experience are composed of exactly "those bodily changes which we ordinarily call their expression."

Emotions are instinctive: fear and aggression cause physical and chemical changes in our bodies, such as an altered heartbeat, faster breathing, difficulty sleeping, or indigestion. Basically, emotion is not possible without physical sensation. Even physical pain—like a stomachache, for instance—will be exhibited through facial expressions and body language. These are emotions that we cannot control, but for those that we can control, we can rely on logic to help us get over them. Society teaches us to allow logic to discipline emotions. While logic helps control how we feel, suppressing emotional response is both difficult and unhealthy.

Moreover, emotions are created in the amygdala, located in the deep center of the limbic system. The emotional brain or limbic brain communicates in images, metaphors, and emotions.

Figure 14: This almond-shaped mass controls basic survival functions, the feelings of fear and anger, and our reactions to social and sexual behavior.

The hippocampus is connected to the amygdala and controls the process of receiving new memories for short and long-term storage. It plays such an essential role that, without it, we would not be able to understand the concept of the present and would only live in past memories. Alzheimer's disease causes this part of the brain to shut down.

Feelings are housed in the neocortex, which is referred to as the "thinking" part of the brain. The neocortex controls higher cognitive functions like reasoning, learning, problem-solving, making choices, and planning. The neocortex is responsible for words, ideas, and concepts.

THE LIMBIC SYSTEM

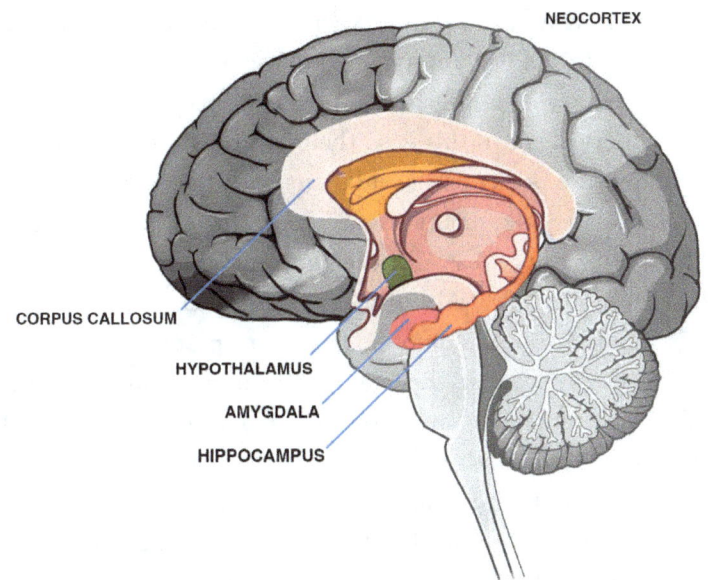

Fig. 14: The limbic system in the human brain

Accordingly, emotions are biological limbic responses toward new sensory information. Our amygdala assesses our situation and tells our bodies to react properly: whether we should experience calm or stress. When the amygdala detects pleasure, arousal, or satisfaction, the brain releases dopamine and serotonin, which slow our heart rate, relax our muscles, create calm, and increase motivation. If we feel threatened, our heart rate and breathing quicken, our muscles will tense up, and the brain will release adrenaline and cortisol into the body.

This process of emotional triggering within the primitive brain system is known as "fight or flight." It is our body's natural defense system that alerts us of impending danger. In a fight or flight response, the body's initial instinct is "flight," or to evade danger by fleeing with the intent of avoiding pain. In the event that we cannot escape danger, our second reaction is to "fight." If our fear of the danger is too overwhelming, however, our bodies can also respond by "freezing," rendering us unable to fight or flee altogether. In this sense, our behavior and emotions are controlled by chemical messages.

Sometimes, the stimuli we experience can affect our ability to think. Our experiences and past memories may intensify our present emotional response in ways we may unknowingly draw upon when we recall our past and the emotion that comes with it. It is important to note that the brain lacks a concept of time, so any emotions associated with pain can be felt just as powerfully during recall as when first experienced. In this way, the brain uses past experience to tell it how to respond in the present. Despite memory fading—like the time, place, and persons involved—the emotions tied to them do not. Pain experienced during childhood can hurt just as much during the present when something triggers the recollection of a painful memory or when your brain associates a current emotion with a similar emotion from your past.

Emotion is the single most important factor in determining self-image and identity. When we remember ourselves, we should do so with neither judgment nor prejudice, only with the desire to discover our truth. The moment we attach an opinion to the person we once were, we risk erasing any chance of emotional development. Only an objective look into our past can reveal that the truth may be the opposite of what we understood at the time. That said, dwelling on the past also hinders our progress. We mustn't get stuck in our old ways, unable to make progress. Just as our struggle persists, our efforts must match them to discover our true self-image.

Taking responsibility for our feelings and emotions is the first step toward the foundation of a powerful self-image. By maintaining self-awareness, you build the strength to take control of your life: the empowerment that helps you to cope with life's uncertainty without getting stuck in your pain. A clear understanding of your feelings and emotions gives you the knowledge to identify the sources of your hurt, since upset feelings keep us from having a balanced mind. By knowing our feelings, we can do something about them to let the hurt take its natural course, and the self-acceptance we achieve can help us free ourselves from all the pain we experience.

You must develop an accurate understanding of your vulnerabilities and life-shaping experiences in order to cultivate your self-image. By learning to accept yourselves and appreciate your experiences, you will transform into a proud person and incorporate the lessons you have learned into growth and positive motion, which in turn will raise your self-esteem, reshape your image as healthier, and renew your unique sense of identity. Not only that, you will be proud of who you are and not worry about who you should be.

A negative self-image can be traced to inconsistencies in our daily lives—the sense of attachment to a steady origin story. We don't know how someone like ourselves should react to upcoming situations. We allow different sources of pain to dictate our moods, our reactions, and our sense of duty. When we know not the source of our pain, we allow it to guide us like blind mice into the present day, even if we aren't in agreement with our behavior.

Unfortunately, we will never be free from pain and unhappiness if we never look back to the source. We will notice that if we build our self-esteem off others' appreciation of our achievements, we will still be affected by hurt and loss beyond our control at the end of the day. The only way to break the cycle is to recall and review past emotions in order to achieve a new life.

Children, of course, are most vulnerable. They are impressionable, like sponges, absorbing all the feelings and emotions—good or bad—that surround them. They rely on the strength of their families to develop, but they lack the ability to process the emotions quite like adults, so they create defense mechanisms and bury the feelings in their subconscious. During the teenage years, the self-image is very fragile, and problems with acceptance in social settings create enormous pressure. These suppressed emotions resurface, often in unpredictable yet consistently negative ways. Accepting this vulnerability, rather than hiding it, is the best way to cope with these insecurities. At any time of your life, openness and acceptance will always bring you closer to your own true self.

The downward emotional spiral springs from fear to loss, and back again to fear of being hurt and then the fear of experiencing loss. Without confronting the root of the emotions and feelings connected with the images of the past, we will force ourselves to repeat the scenes of our pain over and over again. Break the cycle and take control of your life. Accept your vulnerability, admit your truth, look at yourself, see your potential to appreciate yourself, and take the first step. You must overcome this in order to see your true beauty and your true self-image and take control of your life.

The See-Feel Emotions

Emotions are universal, and feelings are our personal interpretations and perceived sensations of pleasures and pains. We feel them in our body, in our everyday experiences, in our society, and—most of all—when we feel pressures on our psychological life. If only we understood how they work and why they show up . . . but that is easier said than done.

The major difficulty is distinguishing the emotions we feel. They are always in our body, but we are unaware of them. They are always aimed at the outside world, even though we are the ones most affected by them.

Emotions and feelings manifest in all sorts of ways, and it is not easy to make a distinction between body and mind sensations. We feel the emptiness of loss, the heat of anger, the constant rattle of guilt, the weight of depression, among others. They might even be manifested in reality—as stomach issues or nauseous spells that create an imbalance in our lives. We use many adjectives and metaphors to communicate our mental state, but it is difficult to find the time to identify the root of the problems or to reflect on the meaning of our pain.

I strongly suggest seeing your emotions as pictures. It is easier to recognize them this way, because our emotions are naturally perceived as images. In fact, there is absolutely no emotion that is not attached to an image, and no image exists without emotions. Think about it: images are always seen when we recall past experiences.

One day, I had just finished a Photo-Image session when my client walked up to me, thanked me, and gave me a hug. I noticed she was crying. She wanted to tell me a story. Of course, I agreed to listen.

A freak accident took her father in 1979. She was two, living in London with her mother and two older sisters. A month later, her mother gave birth to a girl and came down with postpartum depression, made more severe as it was coupled with the loss of her husband. She slipped into a catatonic state. This emotional neglect, amplified by the loss of their father, reflected strongly on the children. Patricia went into a state of deep shock. Her older sisters, at six and seven, unable to provide for Patricia, were left to be cared for by the neighbors, where fear, guilt, anger, and shame followed her. Unlike her sisters, Patricia would not talk or play at all and would watch people from afar as she silently suffered. She blamed herself for her father's death and mother's deterioration. Her mother, too preoccupied with her own misfortune, did not notice the change in her daughter's behavior.

At six, Patricia lost a year of school to appendicitis. Her mother—who had depleted their family's savings—in poor mental health, put Patricia in an orphanage and sent her elder sister to live with another family. Only the eldest sister stayed at home to care for the baby. At the orphanage, Patricia developed an intense jealousy toward her sisters. Out of spite, she would feign sickness when her mother visited and rejected any gifts her family would send. Patricia felt hopeless, abandoned, ashamed to be an orphan, and ashamed to be poor. Patricia went from a good child that never complained to an angry child who felt detached from the world and her family. She became totally self-sufficient, asking nothing from anyone. For many years, she was haunted by the question, "Why me?" Patricia remained in the orphanage for six years until her mother, in better health, came to take her back home.

After coming home, Patricia's struggle worsened. She returned to an unfamiliar world. She didn't recognize her house, her sister, or her friends. She never had a television or dolls. The impact was painful. Feelings of rejection and guilt gave way to fits of anger. When she could not vent her aggression, she fell into a deep depression. As a result of the self-sufficient lifestyle she had cultivated at the orphanage, she felt like she did not belong to anybody. When she started to work, she knew that she had to work for no one but herself. She would go on to become a successful actress.

Unfortunately, her lifetime of anguish culminated into one fateful day, starting with a phone call from a producer. He invited her over to his house to discuss a screenplay she wrote. After a three-hour drive, Patricia arrived at his countryside villa tired and thirsty, but nonetheless ready to present. Her excitement, however, slowly faded. Upon arrival, he made her wait outside his house, sitting on a flat bench alone while she watched him eat lunch and talk on his phone through the window. She tried a couple of times to get his attention, but he ignored her. After three hours passed, her past feelings of abandonment and rejection came forth, and she recalled her time in the orphanage. She pictured her younger self, crying inconsolably the day she was left at the orphanage, sitting alone on a bench too similar to this one. The pain overwhelmed her, so she left without a word, drove back to London, and fell into a deep depression. Eventually, she decided to search for a better life out in Los Angeles.

Patricia found, however, that moving to a new city did not solve her problems, so she looked for a therapist. For years, Patricia ruffled whenever she would see a little girl holding her father's hand. She also feared pregnancy and became nauseous at the sight of pregnant women—a result of seeing her pregnant mother after her father's passing. Through therapy, she found she didn't need to be independent and that asking for help was not a sign of weakness. After experimenting with all sorts of alternative methods of therapy and healing, Patricia's therapist gave her my number, and Patricia and I finally met. Together, we began the rewarding journey of seeing her self and seeking her spiritual fulfillment.

Patricia was already aware of the pain she had buried long ago—and through taking her Photo-Image, she was able to see herself and feel her emotions. A single Photo-Image gave her a much-needed perspective that helped her unravel her pain. Seeing her image allowed her to open up about her fear of losing face and her shame of being pitied. Not even her therapist knew about this. Now, she is no longer plagued with guilt and faces the present without the weight of the past. After she had her Photo-Image, she told me it was the first time she understood how her past made her the woman she is now; she felt empowered. For the first time in her life, her joy outshone the negativity that lorded over her. Before leaving, she gave me an unreserved, authentic hug, which felt very rewarding for me.

I tell this story because it is one of the many instances in which someone carries unresolved issues long into adulthood. It also shows how our emotions are often impacted by past experiences. Patricia had felt it all: loss, fear, anger, guilt, rejection, blame, shame, envy, sadness, depression, and even the fear of death. Some of us have had worse experiences than Patricia, others don't have any, but we can never know the past, nor the emotions of another person. We can only come to understand our own.

Emotions vs Feelings

Emotions	Feelings	Reaction
Fear	Scared	Helpless
	Anxious	Frightened
	Insecure	Overwhelmed
	Rejected	Inferior
	Threatened	Persecuted
Anger	Let down	Resentful
	Humiliated	Disrespected
	Mad	Ridiculed
	Aggressive	Hostile
	Frustrated	Infuriated
	Distant	Withdraw
	Critical	Dismissive
Loss	Hurt	Disappointed
	Depress	Empty
	Guilt	Ashamed
	Despair	Powerless
	Vulnerable	Victimized
	Lonely	Abandoned
Joy	Content	Happiness
	Proud	Confident
	Accepted	Respected
	Trusting	Sensitive
	Optimistic	Hopeful
	Peaceful	Loving
	Powerful	Courageous
	Playful	Excitement

Feelings are thoughts that come from change within. Feelings are mental (personal) interpretations of physical changes triggered by emotions: reactions to recalled memories and images. They are triggered by the physical and chemical changes produced by the power of emotion.

Feelings are bodily reactions to emotions, which are internal reactions influenced by our experiences, beliefs, and memories. Because these memories are unique from person to person, feelings remain difficult to define and always vary. Think of feelings as being the next stage in the process after experiencing an emotion. Whereas emotions exist attached to memories and images or thoughts and feelings, feelings exist subconsciously, involving cognitive output. Through awareness of the many emotions and feelings we experience, we can determine their root causes and respond or react in healthier, more constructive ways that can heal the pain and negativity we may experience.

Let us acknowledge feelings and emotions as separate phenomena. Understanding the difference between the two of them helps us understand our behaviors and make sense of how we shape our lives. Mood is a separate issue. It is not tied to a specific incident in a person's life. It is influenced instead by external factors, such as the environment, weather, lighting, or people around us.

Next, let us look at a brief description of the major emotions present in our lives that can help you remember and identify particular instances where they were felt so that you can examine the image attached to them and identify what triggered them in the first place.

Fear, for example, is an auditory and kinesthetic emotion, because it behaves as a voice in our head that triggers our fight-or-flight response. Fear tells us when we are at risk so we can protect ourselves from harm. It triggers hormones that quicken the heartbeat and sharpen our senses. Fear is our ultimate defender, but it is not always justified. Everyone not-so-fondly remembers a moment where they chickened out of a monumental opportunity. It is difficult to fully comprehend how fear impacts our everyday life because most of its processes take place in our subconscious.

Fear can also take the shape of anxiety, which can come from just about anything that is unpredictable, though financial instability and the fear of saying the wrong thing are two of its most common sources. Anxiety inhibits our ability to think logically, which in turn results in irrational thoughts and actions. We imagine disaster situations, we overthink our problems, and we forget our good lives. We go so far as to acknowledge that we might be exaggerating some of our fears and yet live on the constant edge.

Loss, on the other hand, is a visual and kinesthetic emotion, which means we literally see the absence of something we've lost and feel it in us. Loss is one of the most easily identifiable emotions: you can see the empty spaces where what you had once was, whether an item, a pet, or a person, and that feels like a hole in your body that cannot be filled. You can only count on the support of others to help you during these times. For this reason, loss can often bring communities and families together. No matter what, it requires substantial coping. Mourning is a necessary grieving period that gives way to rebuilding. If we didn't mourn, we wouldn't be able to heal.

Like loss, *anger* is also a visual and kinesthetic emotion. When we see something that upsets us deeply, we immediately feel the temperature in our bodies rising. It is crucial to identify and label the triggers of this emotion, because it can be particularly dangerous. The reasons we might feel anger are almost endless: we risk becoming angered whenever we are confused, offended, unsatisfied, impatient or disappointed; when we're hurt, wronged, rejected, or judged; when we are inconvenienced or something is more difficult than we expected. It can emerge for many different reasons, and when it does, we curse whatever we can and desire its removal from our lives. If you have ever heard someone say the classic, "I'm not mad, I'm frustrated," it is because we so badly want to make sure that people understand we are not feeling violent, but something much safer. Overcoming frustration is one thing, and overcoming anger is another.

Everybody's anger is different. Good anger can be a good source of energy. Understanding how to use this anger—artists draw inspiration; athletes draw motivation; entrepreneurs draw determination—to keep it from draining us is crucial. Otherwise, it will suck the joy out of living.

If you haven't discovered your desired method of anger alleviation yet, you can start by slowing your breathing and trying to calm your body down. If you excite or freeze up, you will teeter closer toward eruption. Don't hide your anger. Express it. Consciously. It is necessary for restoring balance. Expel your anger outside your body.

If you are carrying an emotional wound, you must let it air out in order to heal. If you don't—if you keep the anger, hate, jealousy, or shame in—it might turn into *resentment*. Resentment is the most powerful emotion, in my opinion. It is kinesthetic, visual, as well as auditory. It can feel like a stone in your body. Resentment is the attitude of aggressive self talks in response to imagined depreciation. It will stir up a desire for revenge and retaliation that comes from a powerful sense of conviction that you are right and you need to fix a wrong that has been done to you. Resentment demands answers . . . but not from you. A great quote from the Buddha says, "Holding on to anger is like grasping a hot coal with the intent of throwing it at someone else; you are the one who gets burned."

As long as you repress your anger, resentment will continue to poison you. And as long as you resent, you will never achieve a positive self-image. Positivity thrives on acceptance, while resentment feeds on the pain that we won't let go. Therefore, while we hold onto anger toward someone else, we develop a creeping feeling of inadequacy that comes from being unable to feel better. Feeling powerless feeds your self-image just as much as feeling powerful does. I suggest you forgive the source of your resentment immediately. If this requires speaking to someone, do so. If you need help, make a list of all the people you resent—even if you haven't seen them in years—and either call them and apologize, or forgive yourself, or both. You will feel freedom instantly, and you will realize that your need to be proven right doesn't matter. It never did.

Like resentment, *guilt* also comes from held anger. Few things make us feel more useless and unworthy than feeling unable to change something that you desire to be different. Guilt is completely auditory and is something that we repeat internally, over and over, allowing it to torment us. It feels like unworthiness—being unworthy of kindness, unworthy of healing, and ultimately, unworthy of overcoming. The only way to express guilt is to verbalize it. Usually, guilty people invite negativity from others by provoking rejection and insults because they attain satisfaction in being punished. These feelings manifest as guilt when the opportunity to feel worthy or capable of greatness presents itself, because we view ourselves as undeserving of those great things. It is important to note that guilt isn't universal but experienced differently, depending on social factors like culture, religion, and upbringing.

Shame and *humiliation* are both powerful because they're secretive, chameleon-like emotions that disguise themselves in our self-image. They are visual, kinesthetic, and auditory emotions that you can find if you look inwards at the place you're afraid to face: the facets of yourself you'd like to remain invisible. Because we want to keep our shame secret, it is an emotion that people frequently repress.

"I did not fear punishment, but I dreaded shame: I dreaded it more than death, more than the crime, more than all the world. I would have hid myself in the center of the earth: invincible shame bore down every other sentiment; shame alone caused all my impudence (. . .) I felt no dread but that of being detected, of being publicly, and to my face, declared a thief, liar, and calumniator; an unconquerable fear of this overcame every other sensation."
-*The Confessions* by Jean-Jacques Rousseau (1712–1778)

When we are humiliated, that feeling is often expressed in literally lowering our head or covering our face. Why would you ever need to hang a curtain over yourself? What emotions are you afraid to let others see? We prefer to hide behind our hands, receding into ourselves and away from the good that life has to offer. Identifying shame is imperative to the foundation of a positive self-image.

If you need help, start by turning to those around you. Confide the source of your shame to someone you trust. The courage to share a secret emotion comes with the courage to overcome its influence on our lives. The absence of this courage can quickly be manifested as blame, which evolves into resentment.

In many cultures, shaming is used as a punishment to teach people what is appropriate or not, but it can have devastating long-term effects, like emotionally scarring a person and making them fearful of ever truly expressing their true selves again. We should never, ever allow this shame and humiliation to stop us from being ourselves. We should also never shame somebody in order to teach them. To avoid the shame of judgment, you may project the image of being dysfunctional and embrace your negative feelings as truth and therefore unchangeable.

We have all experienced *rejection* in our lives, from denial by a potential lover to not being hired for a job we wanted, or even not being invited to a party and later seeing everybody having fun on social media. Rejection is a visual and kinesthetic emotion that damages our need to belong and can result in serious consequences. The concept of rejection has been a part of human nature since the beginning of time, and it is unique in that it directly affects our physical health. In the days of hunter-gatherer societies, tribe members who behaved contrary to the tribe's values would be ostracized. Back then, getting kicked out was a death sentence: alone, the wild was dangerous. As a defense mechanism to prevent abandonment, early humans developed a fear of rejection as a means for their bodies to tell them when they were not acting in a way that would help them to survive. Tribe members who could easily detect rejection would be able to quickly correct their behavior and ensure their survival. Later, the Greeks—and especially the Romans—used exile as a form of capital punishment. Much like the hunter-gatherers, an exile from the Roman empire was also a near-certain death sentence, and it was the fear of rejection that was enough to convince many Romans to follow the law of the land.

We live in a society where living alone is much less dangerous. We can sustain ourselves with technology and food that, for the most part, is never that far away. Still, feelings of rejection remain just as strong. By nature, humans need to feel a sense of belonging. Whether that means belonging to a family, a tribe, a city-state, or a nation, rejection is the strongest factor in making humans seek out this basic need of connection.

With social media, our experience today isn't too different from the Romans. Although none of us face an issue of survival, the need to belong and to be approved is ever-present. We post and consume content in order to belong in a community and gauge our actions according to what this community approves of.

Just as you would feel the pain from a broken arm, you can feel equal pain from rejection. This was proven by scientists at several universities, who found that recalling rejection activated the same brain areas that signal physical pain. The rejected brain is dangerous to our health because it can hurt us and it has the potential to make us even more afraid of future rejection.

We often take rejection personally when that is rarely called for. If an employer decides that your skill set isn't a match for the position, or if someone is busy and doesn't respond to an email or text, you will likely take that as a rejection of you as a person. These situations, by nature, are not personal, but they make you think there is a problem with you. In reality, there is nothing wrong with you, but you just can't see it that way.

In order to counter rejection, you need to focus on your best qualities and understand where your emotions come from. Nobody living their fullest life will obtain acceptance without first experiencing rejection, but they don't let rejection define their lives. Instead, they take rejection in stride, and they play the game of life with vigor. Rejection motivates them, and they use it as an opportunity to grow. Learn from rejection and understand how you can avoid it in the future.

Blame, an auditory emotion, is a natural response that manifests when you convince yourself your feelings are not your fault, but your mind causes you to justify the hurt: you blame others. Just because you consider something someone else's fault doesn't mean the pain you feel is any healthier. In fact, projecting pain onto someone else makes it harder to pinpoint the source. Avoiding responsibility for your feelings is a surefire way to continue a cycle of negative emotions. Reconciliation between you and yourself, or you and the person you blame, is necessary to let it go.

Similarly, *envy* is related to how we perceive others, but particularly what they possess compared to what we have. It is a purely visual emotion. When we look at what others have—both materially and emotionally—we often come away with the misconception that they are luckier than us and that we are unjustly deprived. We can be envious of physical appearance, intelligence, charm, and material possessions. You can even be envious of someone's social status, popularity, or overall reputation. When we envy others, we fail to see the things and qualities that we possess.

Envy and jealousy are the most toxic of human emotions and few admit to being plagued by them. As common as these feelings are, we don't have a clear understanding of them and are unable to make a clear distinction between the two. These emotions can be easily hidden from others.

Jealousy is born from fear of loss and insecurity in self-worth, but whereas envy is visual, jealousy covers the whole triangle of sensation: it is visual, auditory, and kinesthetic at the same time, making it all the more painful to deal with.

When we act with jealousy, we have the potential to lose everything: our love, our reputation, and our friendships. We are mortified when we consider the thought of someone important to us abandoning us for someone else. We fear that our friends will leave us if they become more successful, our lovers will leave for someone more attractive, or we aren't qualified enough for a coveted position, and we focus our negativity on the person or thing that would replace us. We become consumed with the fantasy that we will be robbed while we refuse to accept that we have become entitled.

In reality, people don't belong to each other, and it is possible that someone will leave you for someone they like more. Perhaps you took them for granted and stopped treating them properly. Perhaps your jealousy kept you from acting like a good friend, and you weren't there for someone who needed you. Jealous thrives on insecurity. It causes us to act strangely and mistrust others. This issue comes from belonging to a society where the way we experience our own reality is based on the constant examination of others rather than a focus on the self. Sometimes, we might be compelled to lash out with harsh comments meant to hurt the object of our jealousy without addressing the real issue.

Envy and jealousy—like resentment, guilt, and shame—can be hidden since they lack accompanying facial expressions. In reality, it is these feelings that are most troublesome. They result from the uncertainty spawned from not being able to see ourselves and having to rely on how others perceive us. Most of all, these emotions arise from observing another person's behavior and their positive qualities that we desire for ourselves.

These emotions are inspired by the eye's visual function. We feel ashamed at having such feelings and so we deny them. We often shield ourselves with these "faceless" feelings and as we internalize them, we linger on spiteful thoughts that only create more problems. You may never know how your friend got a bigger house or a faster car, but if you feel good about who you are, you will be happy with what you have.

When we feel *joy*, we're confident in who we are. We feel complete. Joy is a visual emotion that we can clearly see on someone's face. I like to describe joy as a state of happiness that is derived from the feeling of fulfillment. You feel happiness after accomplishing a goal or getting something that you wanted. It comes from beholding beauty, experiencing kindness, appreciating the people around you, and experiencing our human impulses of love and connectivity to the world. It is much more than mere pleasure. As William McDougall explains in his book, *An Introduction to Social Psychology*, joy is an emotion that "helps to build a connection between the body and mind." It demands no special privilege. One must merely see the beauty around us to experience it. Aristotle describes joy in *Nicomachean Ethics* as "the ultimate purpose of human existence."

I cannot talk about emotions like shame and resentment without mentioning Clara.

Clara was a famous actress in her fifties when I met her several years ago. She was a socialite in Beverly Hills, known for her impeccable style—always wearing the latest fashion, with beautiful makeup and hair. Everybody knew her as a beautiful actress and a classy woman.

The photoshoot I was hired for was to take place at her Bel Air home. She lived in a huge New England-style mansion. It had massive windows and sat beautifully on top of a hill. It was almost unbelievable. Moments after I arrived, she opened up her door and invited me in, leading me to a living room. She was very friendly and sweet, but I couldn't help but notice the room we were in. It was very small, and the furniture looked very basic—almost *cheap*. This was not at all what one would expect by looking at her mansion from the outside and from her reputation, so I was confused.

Next to this room was the kitchen, which was big and bright. In the middle of it, there was a big wooden table with some flowers on top. The kitchen opened up to a huge deck and a garden. I decided to go outside and check whether that would be a good spot for our photoshoot, since the interior was nothing short of disappointing. I noticed she had a big pool, but it was covered, and the garden, although well-manicured and green, had no flowers or color. We walked around for a minute.

"We should really go back inside," Clara said. "I'm not comfortable taking the pictures outside." As I made my way back to the kitchen, I noticed her approaching her gardener, who was working a few feet away from us, and telling him off rudely. I thought that was a bit strange, but I didn't give it much thought.

Once back in the kitchen, Clara told me she would like her pictures taken in the living room. The brown couch and plain walls were discouraging. I naturally expected more because of Clara's image. I asked her whether we could see the rest of the three-story house to find something more elegant, which is what the magazines want to see. She told me that the rest of the house was closed for remodeling, so we couldn't go anywhere else. I simply had to settle for this living room and kitchen, which I realized actually looked more like a maid's room.

The maid approached us right then, asking whether we would like some coffee. I didn't want any, but she tried to convince me, saying that the coffee was really good and fresh.

"She said no, didn't she?" Clara rebuffed. She told the woman to leave the room immediately.

At this point, I was really uncomfortable. Seeing the way she was behaving around the people who worked for her made me feel apprehensive. I felt like, at any moment, she would start treating me the same way she was treating them.

Since finding a better part of the house wasn't going to happen, I asked her to see what other outfits she could wear. She was wearing a basic T-shirt and a light jacket on top. She reassured me, "Oh, I can put on some jackets, so I will wear different colors."

I didn't know what else to do—everything about this encounter was weird, and I didn't understand what was going on.

I started taking the photos, and it was clear from her face that she wasn't being herself. She kept staring at the maid, telling her off, and switching her facial expression to a fake smile as she looked into the camera. This went on for quite a while, and then her phone rang. As she excused herself from the room to pick up the phone, the maid approached me.

"Don't mind her. She's always acting this way," she said.

I asked her what she meant by that.

"She's always angry and upset, and she takes it out on us."

I thought it was very strange that she was saying these things about Clara, considering she was in the next room. Then, I realized that she had had enough. She explained to me that the house had twelve bedrooms and seven bathrooms, but that most of it was closed. Clara chose to live in the maid's part of the house.

"I live in the guest house by the pool, with the gardener and the manager. All of the staff, in that house."

I was even more confused than before. Why did she have such a big house if she only used two small rooms of it?

When Clara came back, it was already two o'clock, so we decided to take a break and go to the porch to drink some tea. She immediately asked the maid to leave us alone.

"She hates me, doesn't she?" Clara asked. "All of them do, they are terrible. But, of course, I can't manage this house alone. I need them, but they are lazy, and they steal from me!"

I had several questions, but I didn't want to annoy her; if she lashed out at me, I would leave immediately.

There was absolutely no rapport between her and I. I tried to carefully explain that the photos we took were not that great. I gently told her that the magazine and the public want to see celebrities in their houses, surrounded by expensive things, and wearing fancy clothes.

"They want to see the real you," I told her.

Clara listened, but I don't think she understood what I meant.

"This is me, and this is all that counts," she said.

We finished up the photoshoot, and I went back to show her the pictures after a few days. It was easy to see what I meant about the stiff smile on her face. She agreed but chose a few pictures that I could send to the magazine. I once again explained to her that we could have done a better job.

"The pictures look good, but you look like a different person," I said.

That's when she looked into my eyes, and I saw the real Clara for the first time.

"Sorry about the other day . . . I was irritated by my employees. Especially the maid, trying to get you to have that coffee," she smiled, timidly.

She continued to lament.

"Maintaining this place is almost impossible. I try to save money, but I can't, because of these people . . . these parasites!" Clara said. "I have to pay for their food and everything. They steal all my money! And I don't even use most of my house, because if I open the other rooms, the housekeepers would have to work more, and I would have to pay them more money. So, I just close everything."

Jokingly, I said, "So, next time, instead of me coming to you, you'll have to come to my studio!"

That's when I felt compelled to tell her all about Photo-Image and how important it is for people to find their true self. She was very attentive while I talked. Excited, she said, "As you know, I have nice clothes, and I have makeup . . . why don't we do it now? I'm sure I feel better now than the other day."

I explained to her that the Photo-Image method is very reflective of ourselves and our lives, so maybe it would be too hard for her to do it out of the blue, but she didn't seem to care. She was excited.

She explained that she comes from a poor family. She often lived in one room with four or five other people. Clara's mother was a housekeeper, and she grew up in rich people's beautiful homes.

"Growing up, I always had in my mind that everyone saw me as the poor child, the maid's daughter," she said. "As a kid, I was invisible to everybody. I felt like no one could see me. Sometimes, they were nice, sure, but in a very condescending way. You have no idea how housekeepers are treated. I resent everybody, especially lower-class people, for not having the courage to stand up for themselves. I promised myself not to be like my mother. I'm ashamed of my upbringing, and that's where my anger comes from, and that's why I direct it to lower-class people. I can't stand them."

Now I understood her. She became a star and created this big facade in her life, with a huge house and expensive jewelry and fancy clothes, imported cars . . . all just to show off. Inside, however, she resented everyone for her upbringing, even her mother. All this resentment and anger was directed toward anyone who reminded her of her past, because she didn't know how to cope with it herself.

She went on, "Most of all, though, I remember how they treated my mother . . . I'm so ashamed of myself for not having been able to help her."

Clara looked at me. She said this was the first time she talked about her past with anyone, and that she couldn't believe she was hearing herself say all of those words out loud. She said I was the first person to see her mistreating other people, and that's why she decided to open up to me; she was ashamed. When I left after the Photo-Image shoot, she was sitting on the couch, staring at nothing. I left quietly.

Several months later, I got a party invitation from her. I went to the party not knowing what to expect, but I was quickly blown away. The whole house was open, and it looked stunning; better than I could have ever imagined. The living room was amazing, and the decor was beautiful. The pool outside was lit up, and the garden was full of colorful flowers. The house was packed, and Clara outshone them all. As soon as she saw me, she took me to the side and said she had never felt so liberated. She told me she had found the balance between resentment, shame, compassion, realization, and pride.

"I'm no longer blaming my past. I accomplished a lot in my life, and I'm proud of myself. I learned how to be compassionate toward people I used to look down upon. My anger dissipated. My maid, my gardener . . . they're family to me now. My life makes sense, now. I'm finally a star inside as well as outside. I can finally feel accomplished."

As you can see from this story, if emotions are not dealt with, they will stay in you and greatly impact your life. I cannot emphasize enough how important it is to learn how to recognize your own emotions.

It is crucial to understand all emotions and what the facial expressions associated with them mean. This will help you identify, at any time, each emotion that you are feeling and how they affect you. For the process of Photo-Image, you should visualize what triggers those emotions in you and identify the roots of those triggers. This is very important in order to achieve mental clarity.

Understanding your own emotions will help you understand other people's emotions through their facial expressions when they address you. What you will see in their faces often tends to be an exact reflection of what they are thinking. You will begin to understand that what they are saying about you is a projection of what they are feeling about themselves. This revelation is usually a relief to know.

Consequently, you will develop feelings of empathy toward the people around you. While your new understanding will deflect these painful situations that could be detrimental to your personal life, you will find strength in knowing yourself and be able to distance yourself from relying on the opinions of others. Once your brain will know who you are and what you look like, you will no longer place importance on what others think of you, allowing you to truly live in the present moment.

10

It's All in the Face

RECOGNIZING THE IMPORTANCE of facial expressions, Charles Darwin (1809–1882) extensively studied their nature in humans and animals all over the world. He discovered that facial emotion is universal where gestures are not. He then convinced his publisher to print costly photographs documenting these expressions instead of the traditional wood-cut engraving illustrations of the time. This would become the first published book with printed photos. Darwin understood the importance of photography in demonstrating reality, even though photography was still in its first stages of development at the time.

After Darwin, the major authority in the study of emotions and their relationship with facial expressions is Paul Ekman, a psychologist who dedicated his life to the study of nonverbal communication. Dr. Ekman created an "atlas of emotions," using modern-day technology to document over ten thousand facial expressions. He has also gained a reputation as "the best human lie detector in the world" and was an inspiration for the *Lie to Me*, an American drama. Ekman has written fourteen books, including bestsellers *Emotions Revealed*, *Telling Lies*, and *What the Face Reveals: Basic and Applied Studies of Spontaneous Expression Using the Facial Action Coding System*.

The figure below depicts the muscles involved in producing facial expressions, regardless of a person's features. The chart demonstrates the ninety-seven muscles and nerves of the face that indicate expressions, which are directly connected with emotions or the symptoms of mental and physical emotional states.

FACIAL EXPRESSIONS

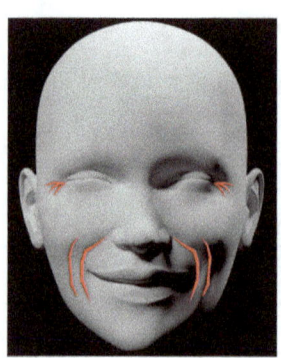

happy

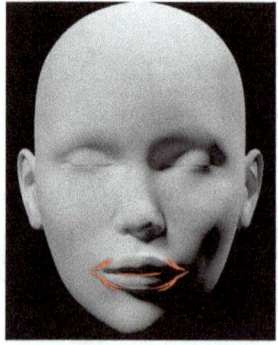

frustrated

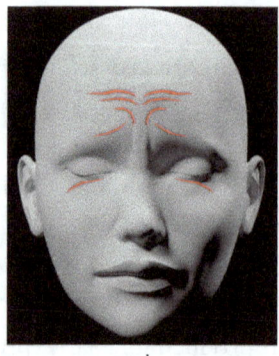

sad

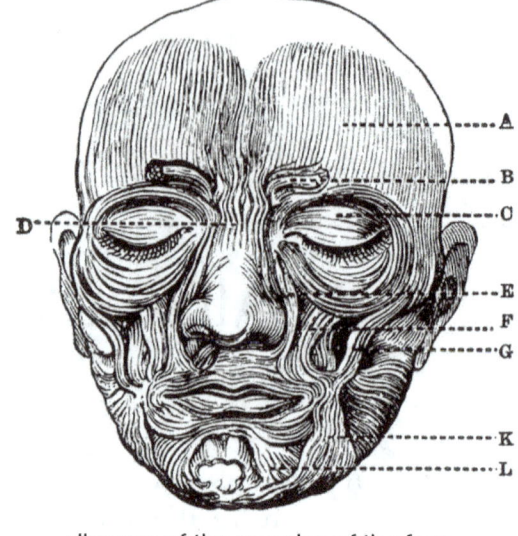

diagram of the muscles of the face

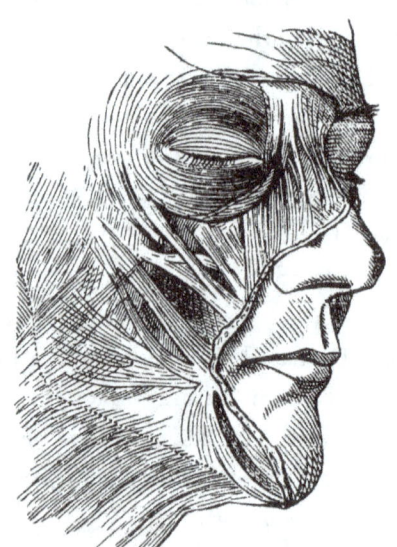

diagram from Henle

Fig 15: Facial expressions
Source: www.gutenberg.org

I SEE MYSELF, THEREFORE I AM

"No matter where you live, what language you speak or what culture you pertain to, facial expressions are essentially the same." -Charles Darwin

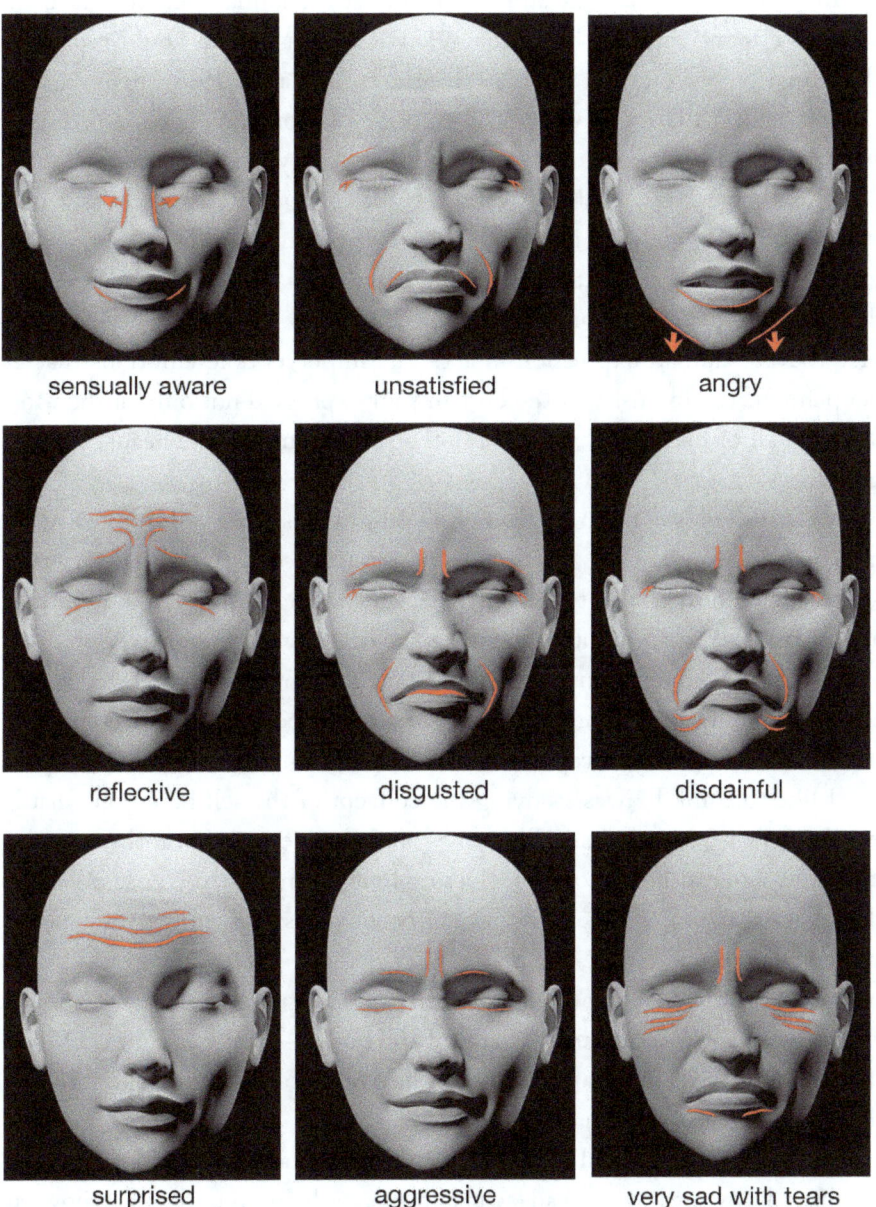

Fig 16: Facial expressions
Illustration: Riccardo Mazzucco

I used to live near Vatican City. Every week after Sunday mass, I would stand in front of Michelangelo's Pieta, staring at Madonna's beautiful face and her entire elegant composition. I marveled at how a human could reproduce such feelings from a piece of marble—it's the pain of a blessed woman showing the worst feeling a face can wear: The emotion of mourning her son, dead son in her arms—and yet wearing an expression of beauty; a masterpiece.

It was then I knew that if I wanted to be any good at my job as a photographer, I'd have to learn facial expressions from the Renaissance masters of portrait painting: Titian, Raphael, Bronzino, Bellini, Rembrandt, Velasquez, and—in my opinion—the greatest master, Leonardo Da Vinci. These painters depicted every human expression in art. The imperceptible emotions that Da Vinci painted, the intensity of the human soul expressed not only in the Mona Lisa but in all of his works, was for me the real essence of the beauty of facial expression.

Da Vinci's notes contain sketches of facial muscles observed from dissected bodies and what are called "grotesque figure studies," as well as a variety of descriptions on how to paint laughing faces, crying faces, noses, and mouths in the most realistic way. No other painter paid attention to the expression of the mouth as Da Vinci did. He knew the importance of emotions expressed through the mouth, and if you look at his portraits, you will see what I mean when I cite his extraordinary ability to capture the true emotion in his sitter's facial expressions. I like to think he was studying the concept of the self based on what he knew about facial expressions. His studies on the camera obscura, the structure of the eyes, and on the notion of reflecting light, along with the use of convex and concave mirrors, allowed him to compose works that reflect the true self of his subjects.

I see the Mona Lisa as an example of Photo-Image, as it demonstrates the unity of the awareness of being with mind and body—a unity of self. Da Vinci's works encompass this idea and can be applied to all of us to reflect a universal feeling of wholeness with the self.

The ability to read facial expressions is an important skill for not only photographers; knowing how to read facial expressions helps us understand how our emotions impact others, how we are perceived, and how we perceive others.

I SEE MYSELF, THEREFORE I AM

It took me ten years on film sets and countless observations of faces before I understood a thing about emotion. At first, I didn't fathom how much happened in a person's face; I rarely paid attention to anything more than lighting, composition, makeup, and the style of clothing—everything I was taught about in school. When I began to understand the necessity of expression, I changed my way of taking pictures. I saw actors imitate expressions of anger, of sadness, of terror, of joy and delight. They practice summoning these feelings until they find an honest facial expression. Sometimes, actors would repeat expressions take after take—once, twice, five, ten, a dozen times—and would go again because they missed the mark, speaking to the difficulty in expressing real emotions within the confines of a scene. This is why I always say it is not easy being an actor. Behind the scenes, I learned that all my experience wasn't enough. My experience would be forever incomplete until I had my studio where I could take photos of one subject at a time.

Since then, I've shot men, women, and children. I studied expression from Darwin to Ekman. If it could be read, I read it. After a while, I could identify emotions, but I still felt like I needed more; identifying emotions was useless to me without being able to understand where they came from. It is important to be able to recognize that an emotion—say, anger—can come from any number of situations. Understanding the root of these emotions is fundamental to dissipate any stress it might cause. Once we know where they come from, we can learn to accept them as a part of who we are. When we understand that our emotions are a natural part of our lives, we cease to blame others and external factors for our problems.

I realized there was so much more to photography than taking technically good photographs. I had to find a sense of meaning in my work. I could no longer recognize people's inner emotions and then force them to present their fake smiles; I had to learn to tailor my work to my client's personalities.

This marked the inception of the Photo-Image.

At first, I would take pictures of clients with varying expressions while a close friend or therapist guided them through emotional memories. When the sessions were beneficial, clients would leave relaxed and happy. Developing real communication between shots allowed my clients to let their true selves come through on their faces. When my clients saw their photos, they couldn't believe that their emotions had transformed their faces to such an extent that they couldn't recognize the image before them.

This got me excited. I began to study the expression of personality traits. I would notice more: the small wrinkles near the mouth, the shape of the eyes and the way the mouth points up or down, how the skin tightens over the jaw when one forces a smile. I'd see sadness, anger, and fear, and hidden feelings of insecurity and rejection.

Noticing Eye Movement

Try to feel sad while looking up . . . it's almost impossible. The eyes are brilliant tools for connecting with emotions. When you close or narrow your eyes and look down, your breathing slows as you receive less light. People naturally use this as a defense—when you're in an emotional situation and need to remain calm, or you don't want to get involved with others, or even if you want to get in touch with your emotions, you just focus your vision downward. When your eyes are down, your mind goes straight to your sad and deep feelings. When your eyes are to the left, your internal dialogue turns on and judgmental thoughts will come to mind. When your eyes are to the right, you become more involved with intense emotions instead of entertaining discourse. If you want to overcome sadness, just look up.

Automatic, unconscious eye movement accompanies particular thought processes. If a right-handed person looks up and to their left, they are accessing visual memory and recalling images. Let us say I ask you what you had for breakfast. Your eyes would go up to your left to access mental pictures from that morning. Looking up and to the right indicates the process of visual construction, which means creating an image or fantasy. If a person looks straight to his left, he may be recalling a dialogue or other auditory memory. If he looks to his right, he is constructing a story or dialogue that has never occurred—lying. He will look down and to the left if he is talking to himself. Looking down to the right is an indication that one is accessing their emotional state. If you pay close attention to people's eyes when they talk, you will get a good sense of how they are feeling.

I SEE MYSELF, THEREFORE I AM

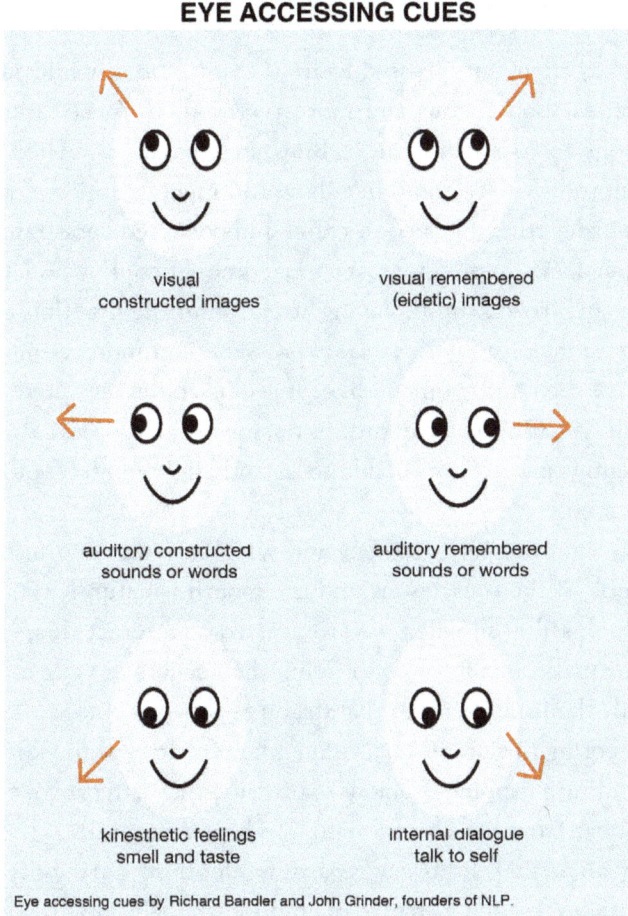

Fig 17: Eye accessing cues as you look at another person.

It can be difficult at first to notice eye movement, but it will soon become natural. As a photographer, this trick has proven helpful in eliciting the desired facial expressions in my clients. Once directed to look in a certain direction or to change body position, a person will exhibit a change in facial expression. Likewise, I can observe the direction of the eyes and assess the person's mood. I can modify my interactions, asking questions or changing the subject to bring to mind happy thoughts and produce a photo that captures true emotion. Also, being aware of the position of our eyes can help us quickly change our feelings.

Changing Emotions

Children convey their unrepressed feelings comfortably, while adults' expressions are far less spontaneous and more reserved. In most cases, we control our expressions to hide our true feelings and remain detached because it is generally believed that we shouldn't show too much emotion through our expressions. In order to exude a cool, calm, and collected appearance, we freeze up or limit our facial expressions. You may know people who have developed a sort of standard frozen smile. Paying attention to the mouth is essential, as it plays a large role in defining the facial expression, communicating the inner and outer beauty of men and women alike. It seems counterintuitive to keep even powerful feelings of joy and pleasure to ourselves instead of realizing these are beneficial feelings naturally available to us and allow ourselves to be beautiful in body and mind.

When we age, our faces stiffen, and wrinkles run deep in the skin. The downward look of the muscles around the mouth is natural when we age, but it makes us look sad even when we are not. To counteract this, smile as much as possible, or make a habit of contracting the corners of your mouth upward. It will help lift the facial muscles that droop as they become weaker with age. I find that correcting this downward trend is helpful not just in hiding the signs of age but in exuding a happier, gracious expression that will provoke a much more positive response from others and make you happier overall.

I made a surprising discovery regarding emotions during my photography career. All it takes to elicit a change of emotion and facial expression is a switch in the body position. The switch from joy to sadness or from sadness to anger is almost immediate. Now, the difficulty comes in creating emotional balance. If I were unable to do so, the client would usually stop posing and abandon the session altogether.

Nevertheless, this discovery led me to question the importance of emotions and how they affect facial expressions and beauty as a whole. We have all seen faces showing ugly or angry expression, and we have seen faces full of resentment, sadness, or worry. A depressed face has drooping muscles and sagging skin that makes the eyes and lips look crooked. Have you ever seen that and thought it was beautiful?

The beauty we project is determined by the emotion we feel. Accepting that our features are affected by anger, fear, or disgust is hard because it highlights the fact that those feelings are inside us. Not seeing them makes them easier to suppress or deny; people don't want to see the pain they feel. Seeing other's pain is one thing, and facing our own is another, especially because beauty and pain don't go together. Only within art is it possible for the two to combine, not in real life.

Breathing and smiling are the secrets to a good mood. As Darwin described, when we open our eyes, we receive more light, we breathe more and get more air in our lungs, and this produces a good feeling. When we breathe deeper, we get more excitement inside of us. A person's breathing can likewise show the intensity or the relief of a feeling inspired by a thought. With chin and eyes up, you automatically inhale more deeply and increase your good mood. You can use this position to reset your emotions when you need to or if you are in a stressful situation. Right now, smile a little, take a deep breath, and notice how much air you intake.

The eyebrows and mouth are the two features that impact facial expression the most. These features make emotions apparent. The mouth is the primary signal for our feelings. Our emotional state is reflected in the shape of the mouth. If the mouth shape changes, we know the emotion changed with it. The area around the mouth has the most active group muscles and also includes the mastication muscle, which makes it more involved in producing facial expressions.

The eyebrows delineate the harmony of the face and a change in their size and shape can transform the overall look. Cartoonists use this to great effect when drawing their characters. By exaggerating eyebrows and mouths, they can easily express their characters' emotions.

You should know that any rising emotion triggers facial muscles before your consciousness has a chance to recognize it. When you think of something good, your eyes open and the corners of your mouth rise before any thoughts comes to mind. The ability to understand emotion depends on the ability to observe a variety of expressions: which facial muscles move, how and if the eyebrows or the mouth changes, if the eyes open or closed. Those around you react instantly to the way you express your emotions. By reading facial emotions, we can better understand and communicate with each other. We can know when to approach someone or not, when to help, how to adapt our behavior and alter our words in a given situation, and how to engage support from others all through first reading emotions.

Try this exercise to see how the facial muscles are involved in achieving joy.

You can use this exercise in any circumstances and at any time, especially when you are in a bad mood and prefer not to show it. Instead of forcing yourself to fake an emotion, gently move the left corner of your mouth toward your left side and breathe deeply. At the same time, extend the smile to your right side.

Notice how you feel. You will feel a mounting joy, and all your bad feelings will dissolve. If you need a good laugh and have a rush of excitement, just exaggerate the same motion. When you have experienced the feeling of the smile on your left side, let the smile overflow to your right side and exaggerate the expression while looking up and breathing deeply. You will burst into laughter and forget your problems, as your emotions are reset to a stable state.

FROM SAD TO GLAD IN AN INSTANT: FREE JOY

1. Lift the left corner of your mouth

2. Do the same on your right side

3. As you hold up both sides, look up

4. Laugh as much as you want

Fig. 18: From Sad to Glad in an Instant

FROM NORMAL TO SNEER

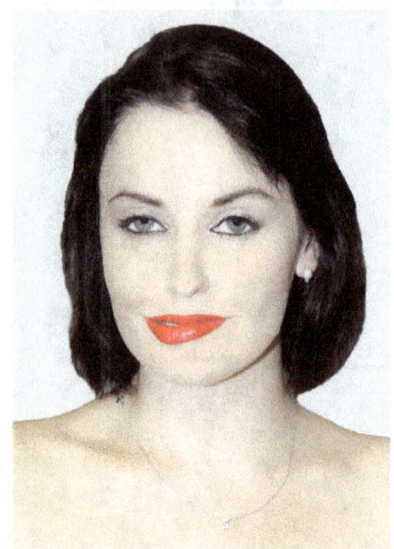

1. Lift the right corner of your mouth

2. Do the same with the left side

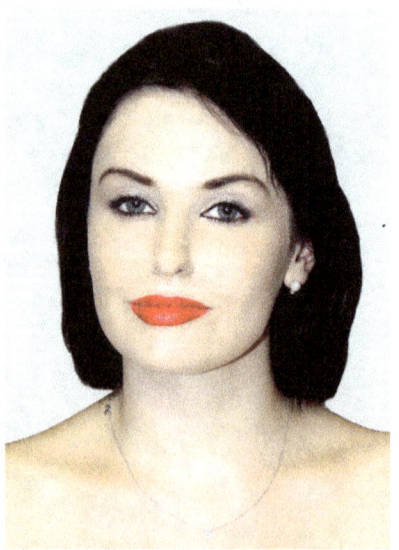

3. End up with a sneer

Fig. 19: From normal to Sneer

Why is starting with the left side of your mouth so important? The cranial muscle that activates the emotional right hemisphere of the brain is on the left side of your face. The smile you make with the left side of your face can prompt a happy thought that automatically lifts your mood. Steady breathing and the muscles of your eyes contracting upward do the rest.

If you start the smile on the right side of the mouth, you will activate the rational left brain, which incites the brain to question the reason for this act and then create a feeling of skepticism. You'll notice this immediately if you try starting a smile from both sides. I have used this wonderful tool to help people unlock happiness for dozens of years so I know it works.

You can use this on anyone, verbally or nonverbally. Remember the mirror neurons? It even works over the phone! Try it with your friends.

11

The Photo-Image Process

As described throughout the book, the Photo-Image allows you to see your innermost feelings in an external object: a photograph. It helps you realize your past, present, and future self, considering all of your emotions, negative and positive. It shows you your strengths so that you can take advantage of them and your weaknesses so that you can work on them. With the Photo-Image, you are finally able to see yourself the way your family and friends see you, in addition to the realization of memories and experiences that make you who you are. It opens your eyes to your goals, dreams, and potential, so that you can finally become your ideal self. It helps you realize the parts of yourself that are in conflict with each other and the polarities of your personality, so that you can resolve them. The weak, confused, and misunderstood parts of your self will finally be clear in front of your eyes for you to study. Having a Photo-Image allows your brain to see you, uniting your self-image with your self.

Let us experiment: How often do we hear people say they wish they looked like Marilyn Monroe, Angelina Jolie, Brad Pitt, George Clooney, or any other celebrity? Think about that for a moment, really. Pick a person you wish you looked like and visualize them in your mind's eye. Now, bring that image inside your body. Imagine yourself embodying them. Think about this for a few seconds. I will wait.

You will immediately reject the feeling of being someone you are not. You wouldn't begin to disassociate your image from yourself, because your brain knows who you are and who you aren't. Not only that, your brain instantly recognizes your image, and seeing that Photo-Image at any point in time provides your brain's mental processes with the visual information of who you are.

The name itself, Photo-Image, is not without meaning. It comes from my understanding of both photography and the way the human mind sees the self.

First, an "image" is nothing but our subjective interpretation of an object. When we look at an image, our interpretation of it varies, depending on our knowledge of that object, and any associations we have. For example, by looking at a photo from a particularly pleasant or unpleasant moment in my life, my current feelings are affected. Even abstract thoughts can come to mind and give life to more or less voluntary imaginations.

And the "photo" is an object. The face, the body, and its posture become an image and your features and attributes can be observed with clarity and objectivity. To make sense of this, start from understanding that everything we see with our eyes is an object, including the human body.

Photo-Image, then, is an object-photo, with Image being a subjective interpretation of what stimulated my eyes and my creativity. For example, if a painter sees a beautiful flower, they can transfer that image onto a canvas using brushes and colors. A painting is a canvas, and the image represented is the painter's subjective interpretation of it. Our Photo-Image is our visual, physical reality. The presence of this image helps us understand that our intuitions and thoughts belong to that body-object reproduced in the Photo-Image and no longer inhabit a phantom world.

Thus, the only true way to see the "self" is through a Photo-Image, which essentially transforms the individual into an object that can subsequently be seen as an image of the self from which it stems. This way, the brain can develop its own objective interpretation of yourself, combined with the clear and complete reality of your external physical figure. At the moment your Photo-Image is captured, your idea of yourself must be honest, because your brain knows the exact truth about who you are.

There is always a reason to take a picture. Friends take your pictures for fun: on your birthday, with a new outfit, new haircuts, or on beautiful vacations.

Consider selfies too. If you want to show your private life, or you want to be sexy, or just you want to show off, there is no reason not to. If you need a family portrait, you go to an expert photographer for it. If you need a fashion glamor image of yourself, you choose a fashion photographer. If you need a headshot for your portfolio, you go to the right photographer. For each photo you need, there is a professional who can do the job. However, when you feel down, unsatisfied, confused, lacking self-knowledge, or just want to have a clearer idea of who you are, who do you turn to?

A Photo-Image is a photograph taken specifically for the purpose of observing and realizing who you are and what you want, so that you can review your potential in all aspects of your life. It is the spark to ignite your natural power of self-motivation. It combines mind, soul, personality, and appearance. It gives you a complete understanding of who you are, opening your eyes to the possibilities and capacities of your life. It makes the path to the ideal self much more accessible.

You might be someone who loves the pictures they have of themselves. If you have a system that works for you, then, by all means, continue to do so. However, do reflect on how many photos of yourself you keep in your home, and of those photos, how many make you happy when you look at them? Please note that photos of you with friends and having fun experiences don't count because your brain tethers your interpretation of the photo to the emotions you felt at the time of the photo. Consider how many photos you have of yourself by yourself. If you have none or feel a strong opposition to having one, ask yourself why.

A Photo-Image is much more than just a clear picture of your face; it includes your facial expressions and body posture. It expresses emotion, attitude, temper, health, and more. It brings the mental image we all have of ourselves into the physical space of our body.

Self-Knowledge and Photo-Image

Photo-image is intended for those people who wish to grow and learn to take responsibility for themselves. We all know that self-observation, self-reflection, and awareness are all necessary for a healthy self-image and self-esteem. However, humans have a terrible limitation: we cannot see ourselves. We see other people and understand them better than ourselves and let ourselves be manipulated by their opinions. We end up with feelings of guilt and shame and are unable to explain where they come from. We have to learn how to pay attention to our thought patterns, to recognize them and be aware of where they will take us—and stop them when necessary. To build a strong self-image, we must recognize ourselves for what we are. We often forget who we are because there are too many aspects of our life that distract us. Most distractions cause negative emotions, pain, and stress.

True knowledge of the self is the most underrated art. Once it is achieved, you bring out the pure creative mind within you and free yourself of society's expectations. Exercising the self is a creative endeavor that pushes us to do extraordinary things and reach beyond what we already know. Once our brain expands to find new ideas and solutions, we expect more and become more.

We are living in a society where we are stuck in the chaos of endless information that is sometimes too much to handle, which saps our emotional strength and the significance of our identity in relation to others and society. It is up to each of us to strive for mental clarity.

I believe that self-knowledge is one of the most important things in life. It can push you to do extraordinary things. You are what you decide to be and what you consider to be your nature. Knowledge of the self is the demonstration of real power that brings out the creative mind. We then grow by doing things beyond what we normally do; the brain is pushed to better itself and do extraordinary things. Thus, in order to achieve anything you want in life, it is a must that you first enrich the self through the understanding of it. You can do this in a few different ways, all of which you are capable of, and all of which can greatly improve your understanding of yourself. Many people are unaware of just how much time they spend in their heads: entertaining thoughts, judging, speculating, anticipating, remembering. Yet, if we ask someone what they were thinking, they are probably unable to tell you. When you practice self-knowledge, you will always be at the center of your being without having to try. You will easily be able to distinguish your emotions and set your priorities.

Sometimes, it is difficult to fully understand who we are and what we want in life. That can only be accomplished through *self-reflection*: when you stop and reflect on yourself in first person. Who are you? How do you see yourself? You only have to observe, without criticism, all the mental activity that calls back the past in your mind, and pinpoint where your feelings come from. Looking inside yourself without judgment, rejection, regret, or resentment is the key to fair reflection. While you explore these thoughts, picture your ideal self. Then, you will be able to reflect and determine what qualities of that self you already possess. With self-reflection, you will learn to see who you are and what you need.

You are not alone, though. It is crucial to look at yourself in relation to others, in order to fully understand how your mind works. That is *self-observation*. With self-observation, you should separate who you are from who they are. You should analyze your attachments to others, observing how you behave and transfer your emotional conflicts to them, as well as the sufferings you absorb from others every day. Self-observation is a requirement to enhance your self-image and self-esteem. Observe how your emotions form and recognize which of your thoughts are beneficial, leading you to behave in a confident manner, and which make you judge, criticize and put down not only yourself, but others as well. After you have completed your self-observation—thinking about the where, what, when, why, and how—try to recall these critical and painful situations like scenes in a movie. Try to understand exactly why people behaved the way they did toward you. The best thing you can do for yourself is recognize the power of self-observation and its role in changing the habits we develop as a way to cope with past negative feelings.

As you begin setting your intentions for the Photo-Image process, it is important to enter a state of deep self-observation and self-reflection. Think about who you are and where you are, right now in your life. Reflect on what you want to pursue, what is missing from your life, what you need to change, and—most importantly—what you want for your future. Think about your role, talents, characteristics, and capability as a person.

The ability to observe and reflect on your existence comes with the development of your *self-awareness*. You have to be fully attentive to the world within yourself and to the one outside. Through self-consciousness, you must search for the root of your emotions and feelings: where they come from, how they work, and why they have so much power in your life. You have to reorganize your sense of self and feel the power that lies in you—the same power that will help you find the answers to your questions. When you have low awareness, you do not understand the responsibility of your actions and make mistakes that can have serious consequences. Ask yourself questions like: Have you been in this situation before? What negative effects became of it, or what results can I expect to occur? Is there an alternative?

Heightened awareness leads to wise actions that reduce the severity of the consequences or likelihood of making a mistake. Mistake is a label you apply to your behavior at a later time, when your awareness has changed. At this later time, when you know the consequences of your actions, you may decide that you should have acted differently, but you always do your best at any given time.

Be aware of the qualities that are important to you—the ones you are proud of, the ones that define you, the ones that make you unique—and consider how they can help you discover or achieve your purpose. Consider the meaning behind your needs and wants. By focusing on this pre-Photo-Image self-reflection, you will feel yourself already gravitating toward your center. You may be surprised to feel a powerful sense of security within your own identity. All of this will show through your facial expressions and overall demeanor, to be captured in your Photo-Image.

Who Should Take Your Photo-Image?

If you want to have your Photo-Image taken, going to a qualified photographer trained in Photo-Image should be your first choice, but therapists, psychologists, life coaches, NLP (Neuro-linguistic Programming certified) therapists, and those who already work in professional health and wellness will naturally be able to help you open up to the center of your being with sensitivity and kindness.

I advise against friends or family taking your Photo-Image, because they may make it difficult to concentrate on yourself. I also advise against taking your own Photo-Image. That said, it is still possible; just don't use a camera phone!

It is critical to work with someone who cares about you as a person, because it will be their job to create an artistic work that reflects your authentic self. A photographer should understand your need for why you want to have your

Photo-Image taken, and they will achieve great satisfaction in providing this service.

A Photo-Image is taken safely in a studio or a quiet place; no props, no pictures, only a simple background with lights and a camera. The photographer should be behind the camera so you can barely see them. The client is in charge of creating the image of their identity. This is a time for you to concentrate on yourself. You can express yourself freely and without judgment, pressure, or suggestions. There is only your body and yourself in your mind's eye, your life, your wishes, and your feelings. You follow the steps that stimulate your reality in all aspects of life while the photographer shoots the photos.

Props, symbols, patterns, and other distracting add-ons should be avoided. Likewise, flamboyant poses, hand gestures, and actions in the shot will obscure the focus of the image. You should wear makeup if it makes you feel comfortable but avoid wearing trendy accessories since fashion tastes and trends are fleeting. Using Photoshop to correct a blemish is not forbidden, but the point is to have an image that represents you the best. This is not a question of looking a certain way; it is about what your essence reveals about who you are. You should dress however you like and pose however you feel most comfortable—most importantly, you should feel free to express yourself and your feelings during the shoot.

After many shots have been taken, and the photographs are ready, you must choose *one* of them. This selection process is highly personal and should be left solely to your own judgment. Only you can recognize your true self in the image; only you can see yourself. In no way should the photographer or therapist suggest the "right" photos for the client. It is your job to know what a particular feeling or expression means to you. Remember that the brain is the commander-in-chief of your experience. When your brain sees your Photo-Image, it should fill your body with the sensation you felt while getting the pictures taken. Each time you look at your Photo-Image, an overwhelming sensation of joy will support who you truly are.

The Photo-Image will reflect your total self—your character, style, emotions, energy—and through it, you will rediscover the person you truly are along with some goals you may have pushed away.

The person you see in your Photo-Image is a new, genuine person.

Picturing Your Dreams

There are specific and important factors to consider that affect the results of your desired outcome, according to Robert Dilts' book, *Strategies of Genius*. The best way to align yourself with your goals is to consider all aspects of your life:

- Environment: Where and when. Ask yourself, what are the environmental conditions right now in your life? What would you prefer them to be?
- Behavior: Your actions to get results. What must you do to achieve my potential to create results?
- Capability: Your knowledge, skills, and ability. How are you able to achieve my goal? What skills do you need and where can you learn them?
- Beliefs/Values: What are your beliefs and values? How do your beliefs influence your life? Do your beliefs/values limit or propel you?
- Identity: The sense of who you are. Are you confident in who you are? Do you behave like the person you think you are?
- Purpose: Your reason for being. What is your mission? What is your driving force?

Reflecting on these factors will always allow you to move forward in life. The result is transformative when combined with your Photo-Image. Everything will be in sync with who you are. The following exercise will guide you toward centering yourself and your desired outcome, giving you a sense of wholeness that will prepare you to take your Photo-Image:

- Feel inside of you a positive energy toward all aspects of your life.
- Imagine applying your positivity to your future.
- Think long and clear about what you want and deserve.
- Breathe this feeling into your body; experience the sense of your awareness.
- Now, you are sure of your goals and what you want to do with your life.

Performing this exercise before taking your Photo-Image will help you experience yourself completely. This realization will be the power that supports you each time you see your Photo-Image, because it harbors the truth of your essence as a being in time and space capable of experiencing life with joy and happiness.

A few years ago, I had a Photo-Image session with Cindy. Cindy was in her late forties when we met, and her life was seemingly perfect: she had a happy marriage with a man she loves and a career to be proud of. She had been a manager in one of the biggest US federal agencies for most of her adult life and was respected in her field. I quickly became intrigued by her interest in Photo-Image when she arrived for the shoot. As we talked and I got to know her better, I decided to ask why she had decided to meet with me that day.

"I know I have everything most people want," she said, "but I've been miserable for a while, now. I'm not depressed. I'm just tired of being a good wife, a good worker, a good neighbor . . ."

I thought she might be going through a midlife crisis and gave her some space to get comfortable with me. I knew that there was a lot to talk about.

As part of the Photo-Image method, I ask my clients questions about a few key themes of their lives, such as their behavior, capability, belief systems, and identity. When she started talking about how she saw herself, she hesitated.

"I have respect, I have money, I have a husband who loves me. I have everything, but none of this is who I am."

Silence.

"Don't tell me what you have, tell me who you are. Who are you? What do you want?" I questioned.

"I just want to be myself. I'm tired of pretending to be happy," she said, breaking into a shy smile. "You know . . . when I was a little girl, I spent all of my free time playing outside with soil, trying to understand why planting seeds make a flower, and watching my beautiful sprouts grow taller, and eventually blooming into beautiful forms and colors. I would show them to my family and say, with all the pride in the world, that it was me who created that beautiful flower, with its bright reds and delicate scent . . ."

She looked at me.

"Pina, I really miss that happy, enthusiastic girl. *That's* what I want."

There was a lot of passion in her eyes as she talked.

I gave her a second and then asked, "What exactly is stopping you from being the girl you were?"

She was quiet for a few minutes, deep in her thoughts. I continued.

"Think about it. What would pursuing what you want do for you?"

She answered promptly.

"I would finally be happy. I will feel that I have accomplished something in my life!"

Several seconds passed.

"But I'm scared. I'm scared of leaving my job and the security that comes with it. I'm scared of failure. I'm scared of losing what I have now. I'm scared of what other people would think."

We kept talking as the shoot went on, digging into the core of what she truly wants as well as the Photo-Image concept and its effects on people.

We finished the shoot a couple of hours later, and I remember she left with a big smile. I didn't hear from her for about a year after. I thought about her often, and I wanted to contact her, but I don't usually reach out to clients as they might feel pressured. One day, I got a call from her, inviting me to come over for coffee. As we talked that day, I could tell that she was happier just by looking at her. Her eyes were shining, and there was a levity about her that hadn't been there before. She told me that, in the next few months following our shoot, all she could do was look at her Photo-Image and think about our conversation.

"So, I decided to stop thinking about it and do something," she said.

She had started her studies on botany and gardening and launched a blog where she wrote about her passion every week. She gathered a lot of followers. Then, one day, out of the blue, Cindy decided to quit her management job. Now, she is a successful landscape designer.

After our coffee, she said she wanted to show me something. We headed outside and started walking toward the back of the house. As soon as I laid my eyes upon her garden, my mind was blown. It was one of the most beautiful things I had ever seen. It was impeccably arranged, and the blues and oranges and bright yellows were beautifully color-coordinated. The scent in the air was unforgettable. Her garden was truly a masterpiece. I will never forget the way Cindy's eyes beamed as she looked at those flowers and at me with gratitude. Her husband, who had also quit his job to assist her in her successful gardening venture, approached us.

"She's an artist, isn't she?" he said, as they embraced.

Every time she had a doubt or started to feel any hint of regret, she would look at her Photo-Image, and it would remind her of her potential, renewing her motivation to keep following her goals.

I want you to think about these questions:

- What do I want?
- What do I need?
- Do I need more resources?
- Do I need money?
- How can I make more money with what I have and my situation right now?
- Do I need more knowledge?
- Do I need to change?
- Do I want to be more outgoing?
- Where do I feel at my best?
- How can I take advantage of what I already have?
- How do I do it with my capabilities?
- What do I have to do?
- Do I want more of a social life?
- Do I want to grow my business?
- Do I want to develop my creative work?
- What is the best way to fulfill my life?
- What is the purpose of my life?
- What is the inspiration for my ultimate contribution and value I believe in?

Don't worry, you don't need to answer all of them; just thinking about the questions themselves may tug at your spirit. As your answers fill your mind, you will begin to realize how your new Photo-Image will help clear the confusing thoughts and the chatter in your mind. You know a lot more about yourself than you might like to believe; your Photo-Image will reflect your understanding of yourself.

Also, be aware that the way you phrase your goals affects the goals themselves. "I don't want to be shy" is not the same thing as "I want to be more self-confident." Thinking about what you want instead of what you don't want makes a huge difference. Make your aim personal and something *you* want to do, not something you want to happen to you. Make sure your aim is within your control. We all want other people to change, but you should remember that you cannot do anything to control them. Focus only on what you are able to do. If you have a goal with multiple outcomes, find a path that connects them in some way. For example, if you want to lose weight or enroll in a gym or learn about health and nutrition, they are in the same category: I want to be healthy.

Scan your brain and try to observe your life from youth to present. Note the beauty you have and all that you have learned. Remember your friends, your parents, your dreams, your birthday parties, your happiest moments. Remember the problems you have solved and the adversity you have faced, consider how these experiences have shaped your goal, and choose the path that you deserve. Remember that your brain follows your directions. If you give it the wrong direction, it will steer you off course. Your Photo-Image will act as your brain's North Star.

By keeping your Photo-Image in front of you and keeping it in mind every day—just as we have the images of other people in front of us—you find yourself consciously making decisions that keep you safe and healthy. Having a Photo-Image of yourself will remind you that you have a body: that you *are* your body. I also advise that you regularly touch your head to get a feeling of its shape and size, as well as the features of your face. Caresses, hugs, and massages give the brain an idea of the dimensions of the body.

The joy that comes from the confidence of seeing yourself as you are, will propel you toward your goals. If you are reading this and wish you could feel joy, don't worry. Joy will resurface after you see yourself, and happiness will take hold once you recognize the steps you need to take to complete yourself. You

I SEE MYSELF, THEREFORE I AM

will become excited about the future. In this state, we project joy outward, we approach our goals with energy and courage and strive to overcome obstacles.

Seeing your Photo-Image is a visual experience that brings joy and happiness. When you are in tune with yourself, it is difficult to get angry, envious or jealous.

12

The Photo-Image in Action

Keeping a Photo-Image somewhere you will see it often will create a physical link between your external features with your sensations, experiences, feelings, and qualities, including strong motivation. Showing the brain your Photo-Image will create unity in your being, allowing your brain to work with confidence in you because you will be working directly for your own benefit. You will feel positivity right away, reenacting what you felt when the picture was taken. You will be able to direct your energy with an overwhelming feeling of self-love.

As previously mentioned, a portrait or a snapshot is not enough for you to be able to see yourself. Your mirror image, your circumstantial photos, your opinion on others' opinions about your appearance, and your self-image that you have based on these things were, until now, shadowy and unclear.

Consider how many images of yourself you can conjure in your brain and the different roles you take on in each of them—family, professional, romantic, etc. All these different images and their identities keep you from seeing the real you. Because you have varying touchstones for your identity, it is only natural that self-doubt, anxiety, lack of confidence, depression, and the big question of your true identity often take over. Until you integrate your real image into your brain's self-consciousness, you will never feel like you know who you are.

As the world knows, the brain needs to see whatever object is in front of it in order to make sense of it and understand what it is. While our brain knows who we are in an intangible way—what we feel, what we think, etc.—what is missing is a concrete object to which it can apply its knowledge of self. No ordinary photograph is intentional enough for that: not a wedding photo, or a yearbook portrait, or even a Time magazine cover. This is why you need a Photo-Image. It is the logical representation of your body to your brain.

When you understand your Photo-Image, you no longer rely on what others think of you because you will have a clear self-image in your mind. When you see your face, you see a person with a name and an identity. You see two bright eyes that look back with recognition. You may think, "That person is me. I feel it. I see myself. I can see who I am, therefore, I exist. I'm alive. I'm ready to experience my life."

The image of the visual self that the brain interprets activates the instinctive driving force that gives you the will to act and accomplish your desires.

The proof of what the Photo-Image can do for you is in its results. The most direct way of learning how seeing your visual self can change your life is by putting it to the test. Seeing your visual self will reveal the truth about you, and it will also inspire you to do the best for yourself. To achieve your desired outcome, it helps to think about what you want at this point in your life. We all want to be happy, but we dig deeper and ask yourself what that really means.

To most people, happiness is obtaining certain things: money, love, success, or power. To others, it is living with certain values, like honesty, generosity, and morality. For many, it is a combination of both. We all know what we want and what isn't enough. Asking yourself what you want gives you a place to start from and helps pinpoint a direction that is right for you.

Your Photo-Image represents your best self. When you see your best self, you will feel motivated to act in line with that person. You will be able to rebuff sadness, laziness, depression, and all the negative energy your false sense of self may send your way. This allows you to see what you are missing and guides you toward personal fulfillment. It enlightens you on the areas in your life that you desire to change, and it instills an overwhelming assurance that you can accomplish anything. A Photo-Image captures the intensity of your true self, shining in the connection between your body and mind, thus revealing your genuine beauty.

You will feel your power every time you look at your Photo-Image.

I was once friends with a young actor—a divorcee whose child was my son's playmate. One year, he invited our family for Easter vacation in Hawaii. On Easter day, we left the kids with their babysitter and lounged at one of Hawaii's most beautiful hotels, where we feasted for hours on the most lavish brunch buffet I had ever seen. He ate so much, but I was a close competitor! Yet, as I reached my limit, I noticed he showed no signs of slowing down. I also noticed that he made several trips to the bathroom and every time he returned, he'd eat with the same intensity as when we first sat down.

By now, I was stuffed, so I asked him, "Where are you putting all this food? I'm going to burst!"

He leaned in and told me, "Pina, this is the best hotel since there are no stalls in the bathrooms. They're each private rooms. It's great."

I leaned back, confused by his statement, first of all, because my then limited English didn't allow me to understand what "stalls" were. Secondly, I didn't see what could be so great about a private bathroom. I pretended to understand him and dropped the subject. We enjoyed a great vacation. and I soon forgot all about the strange statement. A couple of months later, we were scheduled to have a photoshoot for an Italian magazine. It was after the shoot that I asked him for a favor. I wanted to compare the Photo-Image process with a regular photoshoot in order to understand the difference. He was curious and agreed, and I took his Photo-Image.

Three or four months later, we saw each other again at our kids' soccer practice. He said this to me.

"I don't know how to tell you this, but your Photo-Image has really helped me. I did what you asked me to do and put it on my desk so that I could look at it often. When I looked at it, I felt ashamed and unhappy with myself, but I kept going back to it to find out why. I even compared it to the other shots you took of me. I saw two different people! Then, I realized that I had been cheating myself. I had been abusing my body, because I was insecure. I couldn't hide my problems from myself, anymore. I had an eating disorder, but, now, every time I look at it, I don't feel like putting my body through what I have been. That's helped me to learn what changes I can make to keep myself healthy. When I hold the image in front of me, I'm reminded that I have to have respect for the person in the photo. I have to be the best person I can, for my sake and for my son."

As the story shows, your Photo-Image has a tremendous effect on your life. When you look at your Photo-Image, you develop a subjective interpretation of your identity—and not anyone else's—which becomes your own opinion of yourself. Having your image in front of you will give you the self-respect that prompts you to do the right things for yourself. Your Photo-Image will lead you wherever you wish to go, because it is a constant reminder of your potential.

One of the reasons your Photo-Image has such a major impact on you is that you are not used to thinking about your identity as a visual representation but rather as an abstract self-concept the mind carries around like some kind of unidentifiable load you only acknowledge when you feel bodily urges like hunger or pain. Even then, you only think about your body; you don't see it. We are often so busy with our duties that we forget to acknowledge our capabilities.

As I have mentioned, Photo-Image is a simple portrait of yourself—beautiful in body and life, and impossible to ignore. Like many, you might feel like your body does not match the mental image of the character you see yourself as. This one comes with a grain of salt: your height and weight are part of your beauty as well. Your Photo-Image will make you painfully aware if you are not in the shape you desire. Your health and body must be a priority in everything you do. Good health achieved through exercise and healthy habits creates inner harmony and strength. We often forget to take care of our real needs and to listen to what the body tells us. We forget that this body is our tangible reality. We must not forget the great service we do for ourselves in taking care of it.

Most health problems arise when we neglect our bodies. Remember that your body always wants to be in harmony with its needs, including nutrition, respiration, thoughts, and balance of energy. The brain requires the body to cooperate to reach desired outcomes, including maintaining your well-being through fitness and proper diet.

When you see your Photo-Image, you will understand what your body needs and what exactly is right for it. Some things you can change with good eating habits and exercise, and some things you can't. You can photoshop out a blemish or a scar and embellish your look with fancy clothes, but you won't change reality. If you are not tall, all the money in the world can't make you grow. It is best to realize the uniqueness of your body and focus on accepting yourself.

Recognize the power of your brain and fuel it with only positive reinforcement, not negativity.

Don't pay attention to what others think. Don't try to imitate anyone. Your style, your life, and your happiness are your creations. Only you know what is best for you. During this time, the most important thing to remember is that you have the right to pursue your path, because you act under self-guidance.

The clearer your image is in front of you, the more your attention focuses on what you see, and you will recognize that the success you seek is already within you. The desire to achieve what you want is strengthened, and if you keep yourself focused on your image, your desire will not crumble. What you think is what you produce. Once you have a clear image of what you want and a strong commitment to achieving it, nothing can stop you.

Seeing your image in front of you will align your thoughts and feelings, and give your brain the power it needs to obtain what you want. Don't get distracted trying to please other people. Believe that you are always doing something extraordinary and *feel* this in your body.

Seeing Yourself

You will find that your Photo-Image will reveal the potential in your life that you may have buried or given up on. From there, you will find the motivation to pursue those goals. It may seem a little hard to believe at first, but a true Photo-Image will fill you with inspiration every time you look at it, and you will feel like an important person in the world.

We become attached to the Photo-Image because of our need to be real and compact. Figuring out who we want to be and what our aspirations are is no longer an abstract torment. The Photo-Image represents not only the truth of your physical body, but also the essence of yourself. It is important to have that image in front of our eyes to which we can attribute our whole being, and that gives us the willpower to realize our ultimate dreams.

Every time you look at your Photo-Image, your brain will link itself to your physical self and be able to recognize who you are, activating your self-awareness.

It is in no way about ego, nor is it a short-cut to success. A Photo-Image makes us feel excited to be alive, for we rediscover our emotions, our passions, and our reality, making our direction and goals crystal clear. It also helps us see what our real emotions are, and which ones do not belong to us so that we can reject them.

Finding yourself does not mean you must become a recluse. With self-awareness, you can look at your image as a secure port, anchoring you to reality. You will see yourself at a distance, you will recognize your image in your totality, and you will love it!

It is true that we are afraid of understanding ourselves because this may require personal growth and change, and change can be scary. You might fear that your status will change or people around you will resent the change in you. Nonetheless, the outcome of the Photo-Image is positive. Seeing your true image brings you satisfaction and overall joy.

With your Photo-Image, you will see *your* needs and desires, and your brain will work for you and infuse you with the knowledge. Decision-making will become easier. Your mental processes will expand, and your opportunities will increase. Your creativity will blossom in the direction that is best for you.

Your image awakens you to your best qualities, along with those you wish to enhance or correct. Everybody asks themselves where to go, what to eat, what to do, how to behave, etc. As you become aware of yourself, your answer will become clear as you see your potential in full. Knowing your true self, you will feel more alive than ever! This will affect the way that others perceive you and, thus, with newfound confidence and self-love, gaining respect and trust from others will become easier.

Obtaining your Photo-Image—the image of your true self—is a revealing and rewarding process that will set you on a path of understanding and appreciating who you are. Each and every time you look at your Photo-Image, you will associate it with the moment you took it. It will remind you of the full-felt sense of self-awareness reflected by your desires, goals, and purpose in life. This self-awareness is what your brain will associate itself with when it looks at your Photo-Image: the symbol of your presence, alive, thinking, capable of achieving unbelievable things. An undeniable feeling of joy is the culmination of the Photo-Image.

Having a clear self-image, rooted in self-perception and free from the shadows of other people's opinions and a dependency on external validation, is the missing link to harmonizing your relation to the world, your past, your innermost goals and desires, and your physical and mental capacities. The Photo-Image is the tool through which you can achieve this link. By seeing yourself, understanding your emotions, dimming the light on a negative past, and gaining insight into others' communication styles, you will reach the state of self-knowledge and self-acceptance necessary to pursue your dreams with confidence and direction. This can only be achieved through seeing yourself, beyond the illusion of the mirror, beyond the fantastical realm of virtual reality, and into the real you. To know yourself, you must see yourself, and that is the power of the Photo-Image.

About the Author

Italian-born Pina Di Cola has amassed an archive of over eighty thousand photos during her thirty-five-year career as an internationally renowned entertainment photographer.

Ms. Di Cola started as an assistant to the famous Italian photographer Pierluigi Praturlon, on the set of Federico Fellini's *Amarcord*. For eight months on set, Di Cola developed a friendship with Fellini and, from this point, became one of the first women photographers in the Italian film industry.

She went on to work as a set photographer in over thirty-five Italian films, working closely with names such as Vincente Minnelli, Brian De Palma, Franco Zeffirelli, George Kennedy, and Maximilian Schell. She then opened and operated a studio in Rome, where she specialized in celebrity photography, becoming a highly sought-after European photographer and illustrating countless major European magazines. Pina later moved to Los Angeles, California, to broaden her access to celebrity clientele.

Ms. Di Cola's intellectual curiosity led her to observe and explore the range of human facial expressions and how individuals perceive themselves. Through reading countless books on psychology and the neurology of self-image, Pina Di Cola discovered that our human minds are unable to process our body's image because we are physically incapable of seeing ourselves, which leads us to base our self-image on the opinions of others, selfies, and the inaccurate mirror reflection. Her study resulted in the development of her concept of Photo-Image—the only tool through which we can see the entirety of our being. Photo-Image looks like a simple photograph, but, due to its nature, it is an inspirational tool that motivates willing individuals to accomplish any goal they set for themselves.

Ms. Di Cola's unique warmth and sensitivity allowed her to draw out clients' genuine beauty and establish strong relationships with various personalities. She attributes her success in portraiture to her care, consideration, and personalization in the relationship between photographer and subject. She believes that "the way someone presents him or herself to the camera, and the photographer's response to that presence, is what it's all about." Her approach to shooting portraits is to present people as they really are—as human beings with no gimmicks or tricks, only capturing what makes them special: their true selves. The concept of Photo-Image takes this approach of capturing the individual's essence in a photograph to the extreme such that the image becomes a reflection of the subject's entire self.

Ms. Di Cola has independently studied the range of human emotions and facial expressions, the human brain and subconscious mind, and concepts such as self-image, self-esteem, and self-identity. Through attending numerous seminars and lectures, and conducting many herself, she has explored the realms of beauty, emotion, and perception. Through a variety of sources, from philosophical and psychological theories to neurological interpretations, Pina has expanded upon her concept of Photo-Image through a broad range of mediums and topics to address and reflect on the importance of *seeing* yourself in order to know yourself.

Pina Di Cola lives with her son, Alessio, and divides her time between Los Angeles and Italy, where her family lives.

Olivia Hussey, Patricia Arquette, Jennifer Beals, Penelope Cruz, Isabella Rossellini, Hunter Tylo, Tiffani Thiessen, Evelina Nazzari, Twiggy, Rhea Perlman, Sherilyn Fenn

Mariska Hargitay, Gabrielle Carteris, Marlee Matlin, Anne Heche, Nicole Eggert, Liza Minnelli, Kristina Malandro, Katherine Kelly Lang, Sohpia Loren, Dyan Cannon, Sasha Alexander

Kelly LeBrock, Samantha Eggar, Barbara Eden, Joanna Johnson, Barbra Streisand, Claudia Cardinale, Pamela Anderson, Giulietta Masina, Laura Morante, Louise Fletcher, Josie Bissett

Arnold Schwarzenegger, Gregory Peck, Harrison Ford, Anthony Edwards, Clint Eastwood, Charlton Heston, Franco Nero, Oliver Stone, Usain Bolt, Federico Fellini, Matt Groening

Dennis Hopper, Al Pacino, John Forsythe, Brian Austin Green, David Copperfield, Dario Argento, James Brolin, Toquinho, Ricky Schroder, David Soul, Ronn Moss

Ian Ziering, James Coburn, Roberto Falcao, Kirk Douglas, Joe Mantegna, Richard Harris, Mel Brooks, Steven Seagal, Pierce Brosnan, Mario Lopez, Frank Zappa

BIBLIOGRAPHY

Adler, Alfred. *La conoscenza dell'uomo, nella psicologia individuale*. Rome: Newton, 1994.

Andreas, Steve and Conniae Andreas. *Change Your Mind and Keep the Change*. Real People Press, 1987.

Avison, John. *The World of Physics*. Thomas Nelson and Sons Ltd, 1989.

Arieti, Silvano. *The Intrapsychic Self: Feeling, Cognition, and Creativity in Health and Mental Illness*. Arizona: Basic Books, 1967.

Bandler, Richard and John Grinder. *Frogs Into Princes: Neuro-Linguistic Programming*. Moab: Real People Press, 1979.

Bandler, Richard. *Using Your Brain For a Change*. Moab: Real People Press, 1985.

Barthes, Roland. *Camera Lucida: Reflections on Photography*. New York: Hill and Wang, 1981.

Bartlett, Frederic. *Remembering: A Study In Experimental and Social Psychology*. Cambridge: Cambridge University Press, 1995.

Bateson, Gregory. *Steps to an Ecology of Mind*. New York: Chandler Publishing Co, 1972.

Bell, Charles. *Anatomy and Philosophy of Expression*. London: R. Clay, Son, and Taylor, 1865.

"Brain Structures and Their Functions", last modified September 5, 2012, accessed July 10, 2011. *http://serendip.brynmawr.edu/bb/kinser/Structure1.html*

Carter, Rita. *Mapping the Mind*. Berkeley: University of California Press, 1998.

Damasio, Antonio. *Descartes' Error: Emotion, Reason, and the Human Brain*. New York: Penguin Press, 2005.

Damasio, Antonio. *The Feeling of What Happens: Body and Emotion in the Making*. New York: Harcourt Brace, 1999.

Darwin, Charles. *The Expression of the Emotions in Man and Animals*. New York: Penguin Books, 2009 (1890).

De Mello, Anthony. *Awareness*. New York: Doubleday Dell Publishing Group, Inc., 1992.

De Montaigne, Michel. *Essayes*. London, England: Penguin Books, 1993.

De Rivera, Joseph. "A structural theory of the emotions." *Psychological Issues*, 10 (4, Mono 40), 1977, 178.

Dilts, Robert R. *Strategies of Genius Vo. II*. Capitola: Mata Publications, 1995.

Dilts, Robert R. *Strategies of Genius Vo. III*. Capitola: Mata Publications, 1995.

Eckard, Maestro. *La Nascita Eterna*. Milano: Libreria Ecumenica, 1996.

Einstein, Albert. *Come io vedo il mondo*. Rome: Newton, 1975.

Ekman, Paul. *Darwin and Facial Expressions*. Malor Books, 2006.

Epictetus. *The Art of Living: The Classical Manual on Virtue, Happiness, and Effectiveness*. New York: HarperCollins, 1994.

Erikson, Erik H. *Childhood and Society*. New York: Norton and Co., 1963.

Finke, Ronald A. *Principles of Mental Imagery*. Cambridge, MA: Bradford Books, 1989.

Foucault, Michel. *The Order of Things*. New York: Random House, 1970.

Freud, Sigmund. *The Interpretation of Dreams*. New York: Avon Books, 1965.

Frijda, Nico. *The Emotions (Studies in Emotion and Social Interaction)*. Cambridge: Cambridge University Press, 1987.

Giddens, Anthony. *Modernity and Self-Identity: Self and Society in the Late Modern Age*. Stanford: Stanford University Press, 1991.

Goffman, Erving. *The Presentation of the Self in Everyday Life*. New York: Random House, 1959.

Gorman, Warren. *Body Image and the Image of the Brain*. St. Louis: WH Green, 1969.

Hall, Calvin S. and Gardner Lindzey. *Theories of Personality*. New York: John Wiley & Sons, 1978.

Head, Henry. *Studies in Neurology*. London: Oxford University Press, 1920.

Heidegger, Martin. *On Time and Being*. New York: Harper Torch Books, 1972.

Hume, David. *Concerning Human Understanding*. Oxford: Oxford University Press, 1994.

James, William. *The Principles of Psychology Vo. 1, 2*. New York: Dover Publications, 1950 (1890).

Kant, Immanuel. *The Critique of Judgment*. New York: Oxford University Press, 1952.

Keen, Ernest. *Three Faces of Being: Toward an Existential Clinical Psychology*. Meredith Corporation, 1970.

Kohut, Heinz. *The Restoration of the Self*. New York: International Universities Press, Inc., 1977.

Kosslyn, Stephen M. *Image and Brain: The Resolution of the Imagery Debate*. Massachusetts: MIT Press, 1994.

Le Doux, Joseph. *Synaptic Self: How Our Brains Become Who We Are*. New York: Penguin, 2002.

Lecky, Prescott. *Self-Consistency: A Theory of Personality*. Washington, DC: Island Press, 1945.

Locke, John. *An Essay Concerning Human Understanding*. Oxford: Oxford University Press, 1975.

Peters, Richard S. "The education of the emotions." *Feelings and emotions: The Loyola Symposium*. New York, 1970.

Pinker, Steven. *How the Mind Works*. New York: W.W. Norton & Company, Inc., 1997.

Plutchik, Robert and Henry Kellerman. *Emotion: Theories of Emotion*. Academic Press, 1980.

Rapaport, David. *Emotions and Memory*. Baltimore: Williams and Wilkins, 1942.

Rogers, Carl R. *On Becoming a Person: A Therapist's View of Psychotherapy.* New York: Houghton Miffin Co., 1995 (1961).

Russell, Bertrand. *The Conquest of Happiness.* New York: Liveright Publishing Co., 1971 (1958).

Sargent, Allen C. *The Other Mind's Eye: The Gateway to the Hidden Treasures of Your Mind.* Malibu: Success Design International Publications, 1999.

Schopenhauer, Arthur. *Essays and Aphorisms.* New York: Penguin, 1970.

Schopenhauer, Arthur. *The World as Will and Idea.* London: Everyman, 1995.

Shand, Alexander Faulkner. "Character and the Emotions." *Mind* 5.18 (1896): 203-226.

Shand, Alexander Faulkner. *The Foundations of Character: Being a Study of the Tendencies of the Emotions and Sentiments.* New York: Macmillian Co, 1914.

Shepard, R.N. and Cooper, L.A. *Mental Images and Their Transformations.* Cambridge: MIT Press, 1982.

"The Anatomy of The Eye", Physics Classroom, accessed June 5, 2011. http://www.physicsclassroom.com/class/refrn/Lesson-6/The-Anatomy-of-the-Eye

"The Law of Reflection", accessed July 31, 2011. http://www.physicsclassroom.com/class/refln/Lesson-1/The-Law-of-Reflection

Titchener, Edward Bradford. A Text-book of Psychology. New York: Macmillian Co, 1915.

"Treatise of Painting", accessed January 19, 2011. http://www.liberliber.it/mediateca/libri/l/leonardo/trattato_della_pittura/pdf/tratta_p.pdf

Van Kaam, Adrian. *Existential Foundations of Psychology.* Oxford, England: Duquesne University Press, 1966.

Van Kaam, Adrian. The Emergent Self: The Self and Others. Dimension Books, 1968.

Waldstein, Louis. *Subconscious Self and Its Relation to Education and Health.* New York: Charles Scribner's Sons, 1897.

Wolf, Ernest S. *Treating the Self: Elements of Clinical Self-Psychology.* New York: The Guilford Press, 1988.

www.ingramcontent.com/pod-product-compliance
Lightning Source LLC
LaVergne TN
LVHW020412070526
838199LV00054B/3589